# A MOTHE

*Amy Shirey PA C, LPC*

# A MOTHER'S HEART

## THE MISSING KEY TO SURVIVING HER CHILD'S HORRIFIC HEROIN ADDICTION

# AMY SHIREY

*A Mother's Heart* by Amy Shirey, PA-C, LPC
Copyright © 2020 by Amy Shirey
All Rights Reserved.
ISBN: 978-1-59755-557-9

Published by:    ADVANTAGE BOOKS™
                     Longwood, Florida, USA
                     www.advbookstore.com

Library of Congress Catalog Number: 2020943631

First Printing: February 2020
19 20 21 22 23 24   10 9 8 7 6 5 4 3 2 1
Printed in the United States of America

# Table of Contents

# INTRODUCTION

During my quiet time with God, as I was convalescing from an illness, I asked God, "What's next for me in my life, Lord?" I was really wondering what God wanted me to do in the next chapter of my life. I had just completed an over thirty-year career in the medical and counseling field, and now feeling I was unable to return to my previous position, I found myself as usual, looking for His guidance. He clearly answered, "I want you to write a book about a mother's and perhaps a father's pain, the **gaping hemorrhaging hole** of a parent's heart and soul that occurs when her child is lost in addiction, and what she is to do to survive that excruciating experience."

I know that raw, **gaping bleeding hole** of a mother's heart. I have experienced that gripping terror. I knew what God wanted me to write about, but write a book? "I know nothing, God, about publishing or editing." His answer, "I do."

Shortly after, I was having my quiet time and prayer time with God. I heard Him again telling me to write a book about "the **gaping hole** of a mother's heart." I spoke to God saying, "Ok, God, I don't need a sign because I'm very clear as to what you are charging me to do, but I'd really love the support of my husband." Now, I must preface this interchange by explaining that my husband Steve was truly sent to me by God Himself. He is one of the most accepting, nonjudgmental Christ-like men you'll ever meet and definitely has no problem thinking outside of the box. So, at dinner I said, "Honey, I think I know what God wants me to do in the next chapter of my life." "Great! What is it?" he replied. "Write a book," I answered. "Guess what about," I quizzed. "Addiction!" he answered without hesitation and almost automatically. "Yes!" I said, "But not about the addict or alcoholic. There are many books about the alcoholic and addict. This book is to be about the **gaping hole in the heart** that the mom and even the dad experience as they watch their child self-destruct into the dreaded disease of addiction. It will also address the helplessness and hopelessness, the pit they feel themselves falling into, and what to do when they find themselves there."

There are so many books written on how to treat the addict and alcoholic, thank the good Lord, but this is not the direction God was leading me to write. People would always come up to me and ask, "How's your son?" While I appreciated their concern for my son, all the while, I felt **I** was absolutely dying inside. I knew slowly the life flame inside of me was about to go out, and I had no earthly idea how to survive. I believe God intended this book for healing mothers and fathers who are experiencing that type of pain.

My husband looked me straight in the eyes and said, "Well, it doesn't matter if you make any money as long as you help ONE person." There was my sign of his support and acceptance.

On the day before I talked to my husband about writing this book, I told my sweet Christian friend what God was leading me to do. Usually, I talk to my husband first, but my fear got the best of me. (Isn't the devil sneaky?) I told my friend Debbye that I felt led by the Holy Spirit to write a book on how to help parents whose children were being ravished by addiction deal with their anguish and pain. Within twenty-four hours she received a random email from a company stating, "If you've been called to be a Christian book writer, we will help you." She forwarded it to me and has since been nothing short of supportive about the book. That random email, very strange?

## My Prayer

Now, I go out in faith, and I surrender this book to my Almighty Holy God. His book. I pray just to be the vessel. I completely submit to Him, and ask that He lead me to share what He wants me to say, to bring hope and increase faith to those who feel they are in the midst of a hurricane. I ask that He help me to remind them that they are not alone, and that they are truly loved—with a love that is unfathomable unless we take the time to ponder on it, meditate in prayer on it, and "try it on" and "get comfortable with it." Help me Lord through Your book to shine Your light so others may see that Your love is what gets mothers and fathers through this hellacious experience of their loved one's addiction. Amen.

I do know that I have a testimony of healing to share. I know without a doubt that my precious Lord and Savior Jesus Christ has carried me through the eighteen years of my son's tortuous addiction path.

It has been excruciating, rage filled, sorrow filled, and terrifying. I have been panic-stricken, and physically, emotionally, mentally, spiritually, and financially exhausted. If you can relate to any of these feelings as a parent, sibling, or even as a child who has cared for a parent who has an addiction, I believe there is a message of hope, restoration, and faith here. There is a better way because of the love of Jesus Christ. If you feel you have lost yourself, He will find you, He will pick you up, and He will help you. He will put you back together regardless of your loved one's status. My prayer is that this book will be a vessel of God's Word to help you get there.

In the text that follows, I will use either "he" or "she" at different times to refer to our loved ones with an addiction. This is to remind us all that the disease of addiction knows no boundaries in terms of sexual preference. It is also important to know that addiction does not know any boundaries in terms of age, race, or social or economic status.

Also, please understand, I, as well as you, may substitute alcoholic for addict or vice versa in any sentence throughout this text. The disease of addiction, as we will discuss in more detail later, will rob you and your loved ones of everything regardless of your loved one's **drug of choice.** Some may die or suffer from the use of drugs, some may die or suffer from the use of alcohol, and some may die or suffer from the use of a combination of both. The results are the same. Don't get caught up in semantics.

While this book is written from a mother's perspective as that was my personal view, many times throughout the book, you will see that I referenced the parents of a loved one with addiction or fathers of loved ones with addiction and even grandparents. This pain is excruciating no matter who the guardian might be. I believe God has a message for any guardian with scars from a **gaping hemorrhaging** hole due to a loved one with addiction. This message may even speak to a child who cares for a parent who has an addiction. Just be open to the message.

Lastly, with the permission of my son Stephen, I will talk about a few incidences of his life during his disease of addiction. These incidences will be in no particular order. The incidences are used as examples of how addicts and their parents interact. This book's sole purpose is not meant to focus on my son or the addict. It is a book about the pain and anguish caused by the **gaping hole** in the heart that all mothers and fathers experience, who live with children with an addictive disease, and how to heal.

# 1

# YOU ARE NOT ALONE

**The Shock**

In the beginning, I thought I was going crazy. For my family, the signs began when my son was fifteen years old. My husband and I received a call from the local Police Department at 11:30 pm on a summer night. The officer told my husband Steve, "Sir, we have your son here." My husband responded, "No, he is in his bed." The officer respectfully stated, "You better go check." Steve looked in Stephen's bedroom and Stephen's window was opened and sure enough, he had sneaked out. "Sir," my husband said, "Where are you located?" This was the beginning of many interactions with the law enforcement authorities, an experience completely foreign to me up until this time, and one which completely terrorized and later traumatized me.

The story turns out that my son and his buddy, who was fifteen, along with two girls were joy riding in his buddy's father's pick-up truck in the neighborhood. I think the policeman pulled them over because the girls were in the back bed of the truck, but I am uncertain to this day, as to whether I ever really received the whole tale. But the truth that we did receive that night from the police officer far superseded the details of the joy ride.

As we witnessed all the other kids and their parents either crying or looking very distraught, the officer proceeded to tell us what he found. He held up a baggy containing about one ounce of marijuana which he had retrieved from the truck. He proceeded to tell Steve and me, "I'll tell you what I am going to do with this baggy. I am going to dump it right over there in the grass of that house and release your son to you; but I want to tell you something about your son. All of these kids have cried, apologized, and lamented, except your son.

He lied, denied, and said he had nothing to do with it. You are going to have problems with this kid!"

Steve and I stood in disbelief, but we were also a bit relieved that the officer was letting us off the hook. I mean honestly, we both were standing there with courtroom nightmares dancing in our heads when he held up the baggy. But we took very seriously what he said about Stephen. In complete disappointment and a good dose of anger, we loaded up in the car and headed home. Like many parents, we had the usual discussion with Stephen about sneaking out, dishonesty, and drugs, and he was placed on restriction. But a mother's heart knows an omen when she feels one. The foreboding message from that policeman hit the very core of my soul. Unfortunately, there were more.

## The Guilt and Shame

I want to stop here and talk about a parent's response to situations similar to the one above. How many parents have been through a somewhat similar scenario? How many parents talk about it after it occurs? Do you mention it to your friends, colleagues, coworkers, Christian friends, or your pastor? Do you and your spouse even continue to discuss it after the fact? Who in your circle of support becomes aware? What about other family members? Do you fear that if you shared the stress you would receive condemnation or might be told you were not a good parent? Often, we don't share because we are embarrassed or ashamed, as if our child's or adult child's behavior is our fault.

We often take on **his** behavior which **we** have not chosen as if it is **our** behavior or **our** fault. Even though my son was fifteen, **he** made the choice to sneak out and use or not use marijuana. I had certainly taught him not to choose those things. As a parent, it is at the very point that they make these choices that we realize we are **NOT** in control. If you feel you are responsible for your child's decision, the shame or guilt you might feel will deeply interfere with

**your** ability to further parent. But most importantly, it will interfere with **your** spiritual walk and **your loved one's** healing. If you are feeling condemnation, this is important to discuss. It will railroad your ability to deal with your child's addiction and your mental, emotional, and spiritual health. Condemnation does not come from God.

Perhaps there are some things you feel you could or should have done better as a parent, but blaming or shaming yourself for your child's or adult child's behavior at this point is detrimental in so many ways. Write down what you are specifically thinking that you feel you did wrong as a parent, and take it to the Lord in prayer and ask for forgiveness. Jesus Christ died for our sins. There is no such thing as a perfect parent. You must deal with this guilt; otherwise you will stay stuck in this deceptive cycle right where the devil wants you. Meanwhile, the evil one can continue his dangerous dance with your child-right down this destructive path of addiction.

Stephen's decision, albeit he was fifteen, to sneak out and smoke or not smoke marijuana was **his** choice. If any parent feels overwhelmed with guilt or shame, that is a spiritual problem between that person and God. If you are a believer of Jesus Christ, He set you free of condemnation.

*There is therefore now no condemnation to them which are in Christ Jesus, who walk not after the flesh, but after the Spirit. For the law of the Spirit of life in Christ Jesus hath made me free from the law of sin and death. (Romans 8:1-2 KJV)*

God cleansed you and rid you of your guilt. So, if you feel guilt, that is coming from the spirit of deception. Don't allow that to continue! Immediately get down on your knees and ask God to show you **Truth**. Ask Him to show you that you are loved as a child of God and forgiveness is yours for the taking, and you can be cleansed of guilt and shame.

Certainly, most parents have discussed not sneaking out and not using drugs. And some parents have talked the talk but not walked the walk. In other words, they have told their children, "Don't drink or use drugs," yet their children have witnessed their parents doing just that. This is not a judgement. I will honestly say I likely fell into this category. When Stephen was growing up, I educated him on the dangers of using drugs and underage drinking, but I certainly had a glass of wine or two after a difficult week at work. If I am totally honest, I will say he likely saw me a bit tipsy. I used drinking wine as a stress reliever while raising four kids and working two jobs. I am not proud of this fact, but I am writing this book in total honesty. This was in the beginning of my long journey, long before I fell down on my face before God in humble despair as I feared for my son's life. So, as you probably know, children often see and experience discrepancies as my son did. Their parents perhaps deem their behavior harmless since they themselves are not addicts or alcoholics. They are working, functioning, stressed out adults making poor decisions. I am sharing this in 20/20 hindsight, or Monday morning quarterback style, if you will.

If I could go back, would I be a complete nondrinker so that my son now would be clean and sober? First, I wish it were that easy. Although there were healthier ways to deal with stress than drinking, I don't believe based on what I know medically, that my not drinking would have prevented my son from having the genetic disease of addiction. (Yes, I said genetic disease, and I will discuss this in detail soon, but for now let's carry on.) However, it may have possibly delayed his exposure and that could have impacted him in a positive manner. It may have made me a better, more credible mentor for him when I later tried to talk to him about the disease of addiction. Instead, witnessing my drinking may have given him fuel to fight back. And, when he became an adult and was of drinking age, he could say, and in fact he did say things like, "Well, you drank!" The last thing we want to do is give our loved one fuel to fight us instead of using precious time and energy to look inside and deal with what is going on with their disease.

And what about the parents that never got up the courage to talk to their kids? Maybe they felt their kids would never use. Or perhaps they felt their kids never ran in those circles. You may feel guilt that you naively or subconsciously denied these issues. This is not uncommon. Perhaps you had an alcoholic parent and were in denial that it could happen in your family. Perhaps you arrogantly felt you were too good of a parent to let this happen. If there is any reason that you feel you fell short, get down on your knees right now and ask God for forgiveness for anything that you feel you did in error as a parent.

We as parents are not perfect and are doing the best we can. Thank God He is merciful and forgiving. If you have just found out that your under-aged child is drinking or using drugs, or have come to understand that your adult child has an addiction to drugs or alcohol, don't close your eyes and don't beat yourself up. Get down on your knees and ask God for guidance.

## The Judgement

Now, this is also a vital factor to remember. When we observe other parents dealing with loved ones with addiction, we can fall into judging our brothers and sisters. Here is where we look down our noses at them if we don't remember that we have been forgiven by Jesus when He died on the Cross for **all** of our sins. As we see other parents struggling with children who are using, we need compassion. Since we have been forgiven so lovingly and so graciously, we should be forgiving toward others.

Be forgiving and loving toward that single mother who has a hard time placing boundaries on her teenage son or that mother whose husband is an alcoholic and thus she can hardly keep the violence down in the home, never mind keep up with her two teens. Or perhaps the mother who was abused as a child and as a result coddles her child with an addiction, says "Well, my baby boy was bullied into going out; I know it wasn't his fault." Instead of judging, let us embrace them as Jesus did and minister to them. They need support. Having a child in the home with an addictive disease is very difficult in the best of circumstances.

Let's get real. There is no such thing as a perfect mother or human being for that matter. But what an opportunity to minister! This is an opportunity to reach out and encourage a sister about not feeling condemnation and shame. It is an opportunity for encouraging her or the father to set healthy boundaries and to encourage treatment for their child if appropriate.

Only Jesus is perfect. We can only ask for guidance from the Holy Spirit and pray for our children as we raise them. When we see other mothers struggling, if they aren't Christians, this is an opportunity for us as Christians to lead them to Christ.

Most mothers that I have come in contact with that are dealing with their children who have addictions, are barely holding their heads above water, and are in dire need of help. They are exhausted, really hurting, and even sometimes turn to taking pills or drinking themselves to avoid their pain, even if they don't have an addiction. They use substances like alcohol, pain pills, or benzodiazepines (Xanax, Ativan, Valium etc.) to avoid their emotional pain and stress and to block out what is happening. Perhaps you can refer that mom to your pastor or invite them to worship, but reserve judgement on your sister. This is not easy as you know even if you are a Christian. They need to know they are not alone!

## Who Do You Turn To?

When my son began his journey into his addiction, I was a Christian, but I had much work to do in terms of deepening my relationship with God. Yes, I had gone to church almost all my life, and yes, I had even done some Bible studies and tried to be a "good" person. But my son's addiction took me to a deep level of trust and connection with my Heavenly Father that I never knew was possible. It is because of my son's addictive disease that I have that deep connection today and a deep level of trust and the intimate relationship to God. It took me years, but I consider his addiction a true **blessing** in my life. I would not want to go back to my life as it was before without the closeness I have with my Lord. You must work on yourself, and by that, I mean you must have a deep conversation with God. You must talk to Him if you are criticizing yourself for the addiction of your child. If you are blaming yourself or putting yourself down or condemning yourself, again that is not coming from God.

He will be with you, beside you, carry you, and never leave you. He will be your rock, salvation, and refuge. This is available for **you**. It is available for anyone. All you have to do is ask! Just ask God to help you, to be with you. Just believe in Him, the Creator of the Universe. He wants You! Without Him, to go through watching your child suffer is pure torture. You do not have to do this alone!

Remember mothers, YOU ARE NEVER ALONE. The most important thing I had to cling on to as I went through the horrendous journey of living with a son with an addiction, was my Lord and Savior Jesus Christ. Yes, there is a lot of sobbing, right? And a lot of screaming, right? And paralyzing fear, right? So, what do you do with these extreme feelings that make you feel like you are absolutely going to lose your mind, your sanity, and can even make you think of wanting to take your life?

## You Turn to God

I recommend that you listen to the song "I Am Not Alone" by Kari Jobe, Christian songwriter and singer.

I use Christian music to help me heal. I cannot tell you what an impact it has had on my recovery from the trauma of going through life with my son having an addiction. I will share throughout this book songs and scriptures that are particularly powerful to me.

*I will be a Father to you, and you will be my sons and daughters says the Lord Almighty. (2 Corinthians 6:18 NIV)*

*The Lord is my strength and my shield; my heart trusts in him, and he helps me. My heart leaps for joy, and with my song I praise him. (Psalm 28:7 NIV)*

When I look back to the episode that happened when Stephen was fifteen (you know, 20-20 hindsight), I now realize that would have been a great time to form a prayer group for mothers who have concerns for their kids due to early substance abuse. I routinely get calls from friends, relatives, and friends of relatives, who think their children have been abusing substances; they ask for helpful resources such as-counselors, treatment facilities, and psychiatrists. But an even greater resource would be a prayer group of mothers who have anxiety and are stressed due to early substance abuse by their children. It is very difficult when your child is young (preteen, middle school age, early high school age) to know if your child has an addiction, or if he was just peer pressured, or decided himself to experiment, or maybe was even at the wrong place at the wrong time with the wrong group. I think that a prayer group of mothers praying protection over their children can be a powerful thing. If we aren't doing this in our churches, we are missing a great opportunity.

# 2

# WHAT DO NON-CHRISTIANS DO?

**Great News for You**

God gave His Son, His only Son. He gave Him up to die. Now, think about that. You know what you are going through. The pain, the **gaping hole** in your heart. Only God gets that, because He actually sacrificed His Son **purposely** as a part of His plan...We can't say God doesn't know the pain we are feeling, can we? So... He certainly can be there for us. But the rest of the story....

He sacrificed His Son for YOU...You see, even starting with Adam and Eve, we humans couldn't get our act together over the centuries; we were very bad at living our lives the way God wanted us to live. We continued to mess things up on earth. Mankind had at starting point, a sinful nature. God sees this and even though He wanted us to get it right, He knew we couldn't So...

God loves us so much. He had a plan to help us. He sent His Son to die on a cross, a criminal's death. His Son was beaten, spit on, mocked, and tortured, and nailed to a cross (so yes, I think God knew exactly my pain when I was sick with fear everyday Stephen was on the streets, incarcerated, and so very sick with his addiction). And as Christ died on the cross, God placed on Christ's shoulders all the sins of mankind. In other words, now, we have forgiveness. Now, we do need to live by what Jesus said.

> *Jesus said unto them, "Thou shalt love the Lord thy God with all thy heart, and with all thy soul, and with all thy mind. This is the first and great commandment. And the second is like unto it, Thou shalt love thy neighbour as thyself." (Matthew 22: 37-39 KJV)*

But if we screw up—sin, and unfortunately, we do, we can bow down, kneel down, and reverently, sincerely, genuinely ask for forgiveness in the name of His Son Jesus Christ. The best news of all… All you have to do is make the decision to say **YES!**

## Steps of Salvation

Get down on your knees and ask for forgiveness of your sins.

**Yes! God**, I want Jesus to be the Lord of my life.

**Yes!** I want Jesus to live in my heart.

**Yes! God,** I want the Holy Spirit to live inside me and to guide my life. It is an internal personal commitment.

It's a privilege to have this opportunity. If you ask me, it's a love story. God had to have loved us so much to give up His Son. I can't even imagine.

So, you see, **You Are NEVER Alone**! Once you make that decision you become filled with the Holy Spirit which means God will forever be inside you. His Spirit within you will comfort and guide you all the rest of the days of your life! We are so blessed! This truth will take you through anything. Hold on to it with all you are.

Listen to the song: "O Come to the Altar" by Elevation Worship

# 3

# EFFECTS ON THE REST OF THE FAMILY

Addiction is like a hurricane ravaging through your family. It affects your marriage, your other children, and your extended family. It even affects your friendships. Unfortunately, this is a true statement.

## The Spouse

As a couple, you and your spouse often have different perspectives. You might be in denial and your spouse may see the deception, lying, and stealing of the loved one with the addictive disease or it could be vice versa. Husbands and wives can become so distraught, hurt, then angry that they may turn on each other. As the heat turns up and the arguing ensues, the chaos flourishes. This is actually to the advantage of the addict/alcoholic, because the focus is then completely drawn away from the loved one with the addictive behavior, which is exactly how he prefers it. He can even get into the argument **with** his parents and deposit some of his rage. When actually, his anger is at himself. And boy will the devil do *anything* to provoke chaos and confusion to readily destroy our families! The marriage becomes strained; unfortunately, many marriages have ended due to an addict being in the family. Praying together is the answer that pulls the family together.

Praying together helps keep an open heart and helps keep the blame away. One mistake that can occur is that one parent falls into blaming the other. As a result of the pain, it is easy to feel anger. We humans often feel anger on top of our pain. This is a defense mechanism to cover our pain, which can lead to lashing out at our spouse. To prevent this, take special care to talk openly with your spouse about your pain. If your spouse just absolutely cannot tolerate discussing the pain then counseling may be needed either individually to express your pain, or perhaps as a couple.

Eventually, you and your spouse need to come together on the same page and admit your child has an addiction. This doesn't mean that you might not be at different stages in terms of complete acceptance. This is a process. However, it is essential to accept that your child has an addiction. If one parent stays in denial and continues to enable the child it can lead to deadly consequences.

Alanon, which we will discuss in more detail later, is a national program that helps anyone who has a loved one with addictions. Attending Alanon meetings helps tremendously to get couples communicating and to get them closer to understanding their loved one's addiction without them having to "argue it out." The meetings are filled with information and you do not even necessarily have to talk while attending, you can just listen. It can also be helpful for a couple to go to separate Alanon meetings so that they feel the freedom to speak independently about their separate perspectives. The wisdom you hear from the other members sharing in these meetings helps you to understand where you have been and where you are going.

Together as a couple, you both have to understand that you are powerless over your child's addiction and you must turn it over to GOD. But guess what? God is **not** powerless over it!!! When you earnestly pray to God to take your child and protect her and open her eyes and heart to God, what better way to know that you have done the very best thing you can do as a parent for your child.

This can be very complicated if there has been a divorce. Just pray that you and your previous spouse can communicate about your child's or adult child's addiction. Pray that you both can strive to always put your child's health first. Recognize this as a process and also be merciful with one another. It is not easy to accept for any parent.

## The Kids

The other children in the family suffer also as a result of the addiction in the family. They are angry at their sibling and saddened by seeing their parents' pain. Many holidays and gatherings are ruined with crisis and drama and financial burdens. Trust is often broken in the family, and relationships are strained at best and often nonexistent. Again, a mother's heart is broken because her hopes and dreams of a family unit are tattered. Our desire for our children to have close relationships as they age dissolves into thin air as we watch the addiction rob those ties. If you don't have this intimate relationship with God to dry your tears, to help you with the **gaping hole** in your heart, it is unbearable.

Unfortunately, there may have even been bullying by the child with the addiction or by other siblings toward the child with the addiction. Also, often there is sharing of drugs or alcohol with the other siblings. The effects of an addict or alcoholic in the family has a ripple effect that can be extremely dramatic. If you find that either of these things have happened, your family and other children need to be in counseling to discuss their pain and to discuss setting boundaries. Don't underestimate the impact on your other children. As difficult as it may be due to the "drain" you feel from your loved one with an addiction, your other children are hurting and may also need counseling for healing, but most importantly they need Christ in their life.

## Blended Families

I want to say a word about blended families. It is hard enough for a biological parent to deal with their biological child having an addiction, but can you imagine how hard it is for a stepparent to love their stepchild struggling with an addictive disease? Can you imagine for a minute, how painful it can be for a stepparent to be lied to, stolen from, and betrayed, while the child is in his chaotic, addictive, behavior and then for that stepparent to forgive and still love the child? This can be particularly difficult for stepparents who came into their stepchild's life late, and didn't have the joy of experiencing that child before he became enthralled by addiction. So, loving the child in spite of his illness can in that circumstance, be very challenging. To love a child or adult child with an addiction, requires the ability to love unconditionally. Only a person who has the love of Jesus Christ in his or her heart can love like this. I have had the gift of witnessing this kind of love in some stepparents with whom I have worked. They have embraced and loved their stepchildren through their addiction, and are true examples of Christ for us all. Even some biological parents can't get this right. Some biological parents decide to cut their children out of their lives. They just can't bear the pain or disappointment from the addictive disease any longer. Because of the lies and the stealing and all the pain, they build a wall around their heart. Unfortunately, that wall will block out things besides their pain from their child who has an addiction. It blocks out joy and closeness to others and can leave that person with a very lonely hardened heart. It is only by allowing the love of Jesus into their heart- to break those walls down that healing can occur, forgiveness can occur and joy can be restored.

**The Grief**

It is very common to have to grieve the loss of natural developmental goals when your child has an addiction. Your loved one is often robbed of these accomplishments and endeavors. I am referring to events such as graduating from high school or college, getting married, or having children. Addiction can definitely railroad all of these hopes and dreams. This can leave you feeling completely confused and disappointed. I had thought I'd be "letting go" as my son drove off to college, or as he took off to begin a new job, not going to prison. But addiction robs us of a lot of natural experiences.

We have to grieve the loss of those dreams, just as our loved ones do. But with His promises God can restore our loses. There is hope.

*Then the Lord your God will restore your fortunes and have compassion on you and gather you again from all the nations where he scattered you. Even if you have been banished to the most distant land under the heavens, from there the Lord your God will gather you and bring you back. (Deuteronomy 30:3-4 NIV)*

Addiction also robs a mother of natural dreams such as her child being there for birthdays, Mother's Day and holidays and even being there for funerals. These are very painful losses that must be grieved and forgiven. Holding on to resentment toward your child will cause bitterness. Again, this is where your relationship with God comes in. He is always there to hear your complaints and sadness and to hear you ask for forgiveness on your part as well. You also must ask for more compassion for your loved one, and always ask for God to help you see your loved one through His eyes, not yours.

God has a way of showing us He is in control, doesn't He? But He does understand and care that we have a grieving heart. I had a lot to learn about my walk with Him, and I continue learning to this day. I had to learn from Him how to really trust Him and also how to rely on Him and seek **peace** in Him. I must say I was very hard headed and strong willed, even dating back to my childhood. I had decided at a very early age to depend just on myself. This attitude was so entrenched in me, I knew that learning to put my trust in God and taking a leap of faith would be a time consuming, humbling process.

And then there is a lot of grief for our loved ones due to the consequences of their addiction. If your loved one is unfortunate enough to get a felony like my son did, that limits a lot of dreams such as medical school, law school, pharmacy school, joining any branch of the armed services, coaching little league, and the list goes on. There is quite a bit of grief to bear. However, I have seen God do some miraculous things! Don't dwell on these limitations or buy into these obstacles!

I met a man in my Alanon group with long term sobriety. He was what you call a "double trouble" dude. That means he attends Alcoholics Anonymous (AA) and Alanon. You see, he is a recovering alcoholic, and his wife is too. Therefore, he goes to AA for himself, and Alanon because he lives with a recovering person. The point is, he has managed to get high level governmental security clearance with a felony. So, never say never!!! God is bigger than any obstacle.

## Forgiveness

God is the only answer to heal those scars and walls caused by our children while in their addiction. As I have worked with families in the field of addiction, I have seen parents that have had no contact with their sons or daughters for years due to their addiction. I have even seen parents who have had no contact after their child has gotten clean and sober, because they feared their child's sobriety would not last. Once that wall is up, it is very hard to tear down. As alluded to earlier, it is only by putting our trust in our Heavenly Father that it can be torn down. You must believe, really believe, that He will take you and walk you through the pain, and heal you as the wall is tumbling down. It is not easy but by the grace of God it can and will be done. As you reexperience that pain in the arms of your Heavenly Father something miraculous happens. I have had the privilege of being present during a few of these healing experiences, and it is spiritually and emotionally life changing.

In order to fully forgive my son for all the betrayals, I had to walk back and humbly remember all that I had been forgiven for in my life. I had to recall that God sacrificed His Son to wipe away all my sins. I knew I'd been forgiven for some pretty horrific things, so who was I not to forgive my son? I also had to be willing to face the pain of the betrayals. It was with faith that I placed all my pain in my loving Savior Jesus Christ's arms and He carried me through. I knew I would not have to face that alone. I worked through this process with a Christian Alanon sponsor, a Christian friend, and a Christian counselor over time. It was a process, a very worthwhile process.

If I hadn't worked through the wounds in my soul from my son's addiction, and the wounds from my past, I would have remained in bondage and bitter for life. However, by submitting to God and turning these wounds over for healing to God by faith, I trusted that He would totally wash me clean, bound these wounds, and I would be free of my bitterness to live a full life and walk in His love!

Listen to the song: "Scars" by I Am They.


Forgiving your child with an addiction does not mean that you stay up close and personal with him as he is actively using and participating in unhealthy addictive behaviors. I am not advocating that. As you are healing and forgiving you will realize you still love your child very much but you must put a boundary between yourself and your child. I had to actually put my son out, turn him away more than once. But to love your child unconditionally while he is still using, means you can still pray for him, and always offer to support and encourage him, **when** he decides to make the decisions to change his life. Remember; we want to be part of the solution not part of the problem.

*Amy Shirey PA C, LPC*

# 4

# WHO IS IN CONTROL?

**Free Will**

As your children grow older, they are going to make decisions and mistakes out of your control. If they have an addiction, these decisions and mistakes are often self-destructive. But, since these decisions of "free will" are out of your control, how can these decisions be your fault? As we have said, unfortunately, many mothers blame and shame themselves saying, "Well, if I had only talked to him more about drugs, or talked to him about who he hung out with, or what area of town he went to, maybe he wouldn't have tried that drug or drank." While those conversations are helpful, many times they do not guarantee that your child will make the decision that you want him to make. He has free will, his own mind, and his own life to orchestrate. Our best work is done when we introduce our children to the love of Jesus Christ. We want our children to accept Christ in their lives and chose Christ to guide their lives.

**Who is to Blame?**

If you blame another person for your loved one's addiction you are wasting precious time that can be spent facing the reality that your child has a very serious addiction and needs help. I have worked with many mothers who actually stayed stuck in the phase of blaming their child's friend, the group that their child hung out with, or even the other parent. Not only is this enabling their loved one to buy right in to *that* theory, she will jump right on that band wagon, and happily evade her responsibilities. Also, with her toxic brain, she will hope she can keep you thinking that way, get you to enable her, and elude all her negative consequences. Don't do it! You are deluding yourself.

We do this mostly out of fear of facing the reality of the seriousness of the situation, and to avoid "shame." I learned that God would carry me through the fear, and that I had no reason to feel ashamed of my child's addiction. Remember around 19.5 % of the population has an addiction, and that's likely an underestimate. The sooner we face this as a nation, and unite together to pray for our loved ones and their families who are in pain, the better!

**Someone to Lean on**

Unfortunately, it seems that taking our children to church has fallen out of style. I cannot tell you what a relief it was to me to know that my son had his faith to lean on when he was out using and while he was in prison. Several years into the grips of addiction, he told me he was pleading with God to help him stop. When I knew he was out on the streets and I knew I could not be with him I could rest in the assurance that God was with him. When he was locked up, he told me he read the Bible every day. It's amazing how he turned back to his faith and his Christian foundation. It is never too late. In the end stages of his addiction, when he was using IV heroin, even though I knew he was still using, the one thing I would do, was invite him to attend church with me. Sometimes he would come, sometimes not. At the time his stepdad and I attended a non-denominational church that was full of recovering and "not so recovering" alcoholics and addicts, so he definitely felt accepted in that environment.

**Letting Go**

Throughout the healing process, I believe the hardest thing to learn is to let go of trying to control. For years, I had basically lied to myself. God knew this, in His infinite wisdom. He knew I did not realize this, in my finite mind. We often think we have some kind of control. I witnessed my son swirl out of control, getting thinner and sicker and more and more cognitively dysfunctional. I realized nothing I had done made any difference. I saw death in his body and face. It was a very surreal realization that I was NOT in control. I hit the bottom. I had never known pain or powerlessness as palpable as this. It was so real, so touchable so gut wrenching, so painful, so eminent. The kind of pain you feel when you are anticipating a death. Very heavy.

I hit my knees, I sobbed, I ask God to pick me up, to take my soul in His hands, to hold me. He did. He wiped my tears, and comforted me. I go back to the Bible where it says, *"Train up a child in the way he should go and when he is old, he will not depart from it."* (Proverbs 22:6 KJV) While our children may stray just as we all stray even as Christians, if you teach your child a strong foundation in Christ, he always has that to return to. If he is already a Christian that is a priceless gift to get him out of the pit he has fallen into with addiction. If he is using drugs or drinking excessively it is still not too late to ask him to come to church or talk to him yourself about his relationship with God.

If your child does not know Jesus as her Savior, pray for her salvation! You never know where God may show up in her life. It can happen even while your loved one is on the streets. God sends laborers to intercede when we pray for our children. Pray protection over your loved one. Be your loved one's prayer warrior. But remember to pray for others and yourself as well.

I met a mother once whose son, who had an addiction, was living on the streets. Every time she saw him, she would put written scriptures on pieces of paper in his backpack. Years later as he got clean and sober and was giving his testimony, he brought up the fact that his mom put the scriptures in his backpack and said, "I knew that my mother never gave up on me but most importantly the scriptures reminded me that God was there for me."

God showed me that I wasn't nearly as powerful as I thought I was! I remembered in my quiet time, God saying to me, "Amy you have done your job, Stephen is grown. Did your mother still mother you at twenty-six years old?" As I thought for a moment, I knew that at twenty-six years old, I was working and owned a home and had purchased my own car. I was completely out of my parents' domain. God followed up by telling me, "He is Mine now, this is between Me and Stephen." I knew that none of the cajoling, nagging, or lecturing or any other manipulative maneuvers I had done, had worked. God was telling me to Let Go and Let God!

While I totally understood the phrase intellectually, "Let Go and Let God," and it fit completely in my heart as a Christian, I would put Stephen in God's care, and then I would find myself taking him back out again and again. I would try to fix him, or rescue him, or put him in another treatment program. It wasn't until my little ole Alanon sponsor said, "Honey, I have to have Alanon and the good ole Lord both!" that I began to realize that I needed a deeper spiritual understanding of how to let my child go.

Listen to the song: "It's Out of My Hands" by Matthew West.

# 5

# ADDICTION AS A DISEASE

Since this book is about a mother's pain, I want to elaborate on one perspective that really helped me with my understanding of my child's addiction. Maybe, one of the things that helped me most was my educational background. With complete disclosure, I have been a medical practitioner, specifically, a Physician Assistant for forty years and have worked in the field of family practice with a specialty in Mental Health and Substance Abuse. Well who would ever dream that I would end up with a son with an addiction! But God is so good. Perhaps that is one of the reasons He has charged me to write this book.

## The Science (of Addiction)

I was trained in medical school that addictions are genetic diseases. Alcoholism was declared in 1956 by the American Medical Association (AMA) to be a disease. My desire is to honestly share the medical side, the mental health side, and to say that even with my Physician Assistant Degree, and my Licensed Professional Counseling Degree, nothing prepared me as a mother for my son's addiction. I believe it is very important for parents to understand the brain and the science of addiction (the medical part) and even the behavioral or counseling part (Alanon and counseling) Those parts are like a college education, but the **spiritual** part is the God part and where you get your healing and life support.

God Is Bigger Than Any Disease

I would like to stop and interject here that not many Christian authors write about the disease of addiction, as if that is contrary to scripture or shows a lack of faith. While I am not a Biblical scholar at all, I am a believer and a medical provider, who has seen diseases daily for forty years. Nothing is clearer to me than the fact, substantiated by the American Medical Association (AMA 1956) that addiction is a genetic disease. It is documented in a patient's chart as the Disease of Alcohol Dependence, Opioid Dependency, Cannabis Dependence, Sedative, Hypnotic or Anxiolytic Dependence or others, depending on the patient's drug of choice at the time of treatment and at the time of discharge.

However, let's be very clear- God is bigger than any disease! God can cure any disease. Often the problem is that we just can't put our minds around a God that big or that powerful. Perhaps we can't conceptualize a God that loves us enough to heal our loved ones of their disease. Or maybe our faith is not strong enough for those big miracles, because we are too full of fear to see the possibilities. God is always **bigger** than our obstacles including the disease of addiction.

For many years, I worked in a private hospital treating alcoholics and addicts in recovery. It's very ironic that my son who has an addiction was actually born the same year I began working in that hospital. That hospital had a wonderful program. This was back in the early 1990's when a patient could actually stay in the hospital for twenty-eight days for treatment. Our patients got detoxification, additional treatment for any comorbid diagnoses such as Depression, Anxiety, PTSD (or any other Psych disorders), addiction education, individual, group, and family therapy, and even recreation therapy, to learn how to have fun without drugs and alcohol. They even went on "passes" to test out how they would do when they got released to go home. When they left the program, they had a Sponsor in AA, (Alcoholics Anonymous) or NA (Narcotics Anonymous) and were connected to an AA or NA home group. This was a *very thorough* program. I only wish we had thorough programs like this for everyone today to help our loved ones. Needless to say, I received some great experience working with the "Disease Concept" and helping people with addiction.

I came to understand that having an **addiction is** a big deal to accept. To come to an acceptance one day at a time that you have an **addictive disease**, and have to live with this every day for the rest of your life is very difficult. This means you can consume no alcohol, or any addictive medications, and of course, no illicit substances, for the rest of your life. However, you can still live a healthy, happy life, if you stay cognizant and alert to what you need to do to take care of yourself and your recovery. It can somewhat be compared to having Diabetes, in that you can live a healthy life, as long as you eat healthy foods, and do not consume sugar. In other words, put what you need to do to take care of your health front and center, and be very diligent and alert. I am not trying to minimize either of these genetic diseases, but as my great friend who has over thirty years of sobriety from alcoholism says, "Having an addiction **is** a big deal, until you come to accept it, and you work your sobriety program. You will then start serving others, and as a result, it then becomes a **blessing**." His attitude is very Christ like. As we accept Christ in our hearts, we become servers of others.

What people with long term sobriety do is simply; literally stay away from addictive substances one day at a time by relying on their Higher Power, and then share how they do this- their experiences with others. This is no doubt an oversimplification but hopefully will help you understand why my friend sees his recovery as a blessing.

Many young adolescents often start abusing substances in the form of alcohol or/and marijuana. But if they have inherited the genetic disease of addiction, they become very interested in continuing to drink or smoke. Over time, they increase the amount they drink going from just drinking sporadically, to drinking every weekend, to drinking as often as possible. Or if their drug of choice is marijuana, they increase their use of marijuana from sporadic, to every weekend then more frequently than that. The point being, that it takes more and more, or a greater quantity, to reach the desired effect (a buzz, a high, or a mellow). This is what we call "increased tolerance." As the disease progresses, the person with the addiction will later not only build tolerance and need more to get his desired effect, but then he will increase the potency. This is when you may see your loved one not only drinking, but adding a line or two of cocaine to his "Jack Daniels", or lacing his marijuana with crystal meth. Again, it takes more and more to reach the desired effect, due to increased tolerance, and this is very detrimental to our loved one's bodies, liver, brain, kidneys, just to name a few. This increased tolerance as you can imagine, also takes quite a toll on our loved one's finances.

I explain this well-known concept to you for educational purposes only. Not for you to use to badger your loved one, or count his drinks, but for you to really understand the disease of addiction, and to have compassion. It helped me to see how the disease can take control of our loved one and how I have no right to judge because my son's chemical genetic makeup is very different from mine.

## Understanding Cross Addiction, Science Again

I worked with many young patients who got clean and sober whose drug of choice was opioids, but they just couldn't believe that they couldn't drink a little beer or smoke a little weed. Unfortunately, because of their biological genetic disease, they relapsed and had to start their sobriety or "clean time" all over again. While in treatment, they do learn that they can't use **any** addictive substances, this is termed "cross addiction." Even if they "got hooked" per say on alcohol, they must abstain from all other addictive chemicals (THC, opioids, barbiturates, benzodiazepines, cocaine, hallucinogens, amphetamines). It is because of their genetic brain chemistry and how these addictive chemicals react to their brain chemistry. They are taught in the 12-step meetings of AA or NA to avoid **all** addictive substances. Unfortunately, many with addictions do relapse due to denial of this concept. Did I say recovery is a process? Some are able to recovery again, but some are not. However, as a mother of an IV heroin user, I also know, a relapse can be a fatal mistake.

Several times when my son was in early recovery before he progressed into IV heroin, and he was using alcohol and marijuana, I would try to force him to not drink and not even be in the room with someone drinking. I would become very controlling as a result of my fear. Oh buddy, was I going to "keep him sober!" Well, God was going to show me! This is why a close walk with God has been essential for me. He reminds me that He is in control.

Sobriety is a learning experience for our loved ones, and they teach you in Alanon that relapses are part of the journey more times than not. We mothers must be patient and compassionate with our love ones and focus on *our own* spiritual health. Our loved ones are in charge of their decisions, we just have to deal with our fear about their decisions. This is really where a strong faith and strong spiritual foundation is so very important for us. Sobriety is not easy so I have been told. We have to rely on God praying for our loved ones as they navigate their journey and praying that God will help us trust in Him and alleviate our fears.

## Genetics of Addictions

Over the years, as I have diagnosed and treated many with the disease of addiction, I could count on one finger and I am not sure that case was accurate, the times in which the patient said, "**No one** in my family had an addiction." I certainly had addiction in my family tree, as did my son's father. Most all the patients that I have treated over the years could look back in their family tree and identify an uncle, or an aunt, or maybe a great grandfather or great grandmother, who was a "heavy drinker" or "pill popper," even if they were never officially diagnosed with the disease of addiction. My point in sharing this is that there is a very strong genetic preponderance of addiction in families. This family disease can spread pain and suffering throughout three or four generations. We continue even today to see generational effects on our children who are dying in unbelievable numbers of alcohol, opioid, heroin, and other types of addictions.

## Not Your Cross

Supporting my son with this disease means understanding the disease is **lifelong** and that he will never be able to drink or take any addictive substances. This concept of never being able to use any addictive substances may be a difficult concept for your loved one to come to accept. Think about it. What if you could never take a pain pill again in your life without fear that you would relapse into the downward spiral of your addiction. That is a tough concept. I have worked with many patients with solid recovery, who have had to make this difficult decision. They had to have a tooth removed or shoulder surgery and they were very respectfully fearful of taking the legitimate pain medication they needed for these procedures. Most of them made sure their doctors understood that they needed to be on the smallest dose of pain medication for the shortest length of time possible. They made sure their AA/NA support system and sponsor were "on call" for them before and after the procedures, and they made sure that their doctor was well educated on addiction. This is a **lifelong** process. Did I say that already? I believe they also need a great prayer support group as well.

It is most difficult to accept that your child has a **lifelong** disease. She will have to deal with this issue and her disease will have many impacts on her life. This can bring about fear for you and your spouse. You must have great faith, as you face this reality and come to acceptance of this fact. This acceptance takes time and is an individual process for all- you, your spouse, and your loved one. Everyone needs to be supportive and respectful, but also this disease process is vitally important to grasp. If not accepted and grasped by your loved one with an addiction it can have deadly consequences.

Now that you as a parent have been educated about you child's lifelong disease, and that your loved one will have hard choices at times to make in regards to her sobriety, you can really understand the complexities of it all. But here is the really hard part, these decisions are hers. Now you know why you must walk with God. As a mother, and as you begin the healing of your **hemorrhaging gaping hole** in your heart, you can be a powerful prayer warrior for your child and for yourself.

As your child with an addiction becomes an adult, hopefully, she will have the opportunity to get educated about her **lifelong** disease and the need to stay clean and sober. The choice of what to do with the information and knowledge about "cross addiction" and a "lifelong journey" will be between her and God. Remember, these concepts are difficult concepts to accept. Honestly, for years, I tried to preach, nag, and talk my son into listening to me. I think, I really thought that I could make him stay sober, by getting him to listen to me about the disease and its dangers. Later on, in my own recovery, I came to realize that by lecturing him on the dangers of him using and drinking again, **I was only making him angrier about his disease, and perhaps making the situation worse.** God had other plans for me.

I did not share this **lifelong** scenario with you, for **you** to take responsibility of the process. NO! If your loved one with an addiction has to go through surgery or has an injury, and needs pain medication for some reason, **stay out of it! It's not your job, not your recovery!** Your job is working on you, and learning the boundary of not sticking you nose where it doesn't belong. You can pray for your loved one, this is where the power lies in God's hands not yours! You can also ask others to pray for your loved one.

I do share this with you for one reason and one reason only. As the parent of a loved one with an addictive disease, you hopefully will be working on **your** recovery and on **your** personal close relationship to God. As you let go and detach with love, and allow your loved one to take responsibility for his life hopefully, knowing this information will help you understand how many aspects of his life his disease impacts and this will give you understanding and compassion. Have mercy for what he is going through.

## God's Miracles

With all this being said about the disease of addiction, there is a HUGE caveat: **God's Miracles.** I still believe in miracles. I know that God can and will perform a miracle any and every day He chooses. I have witnessed His Miracles in my life, unrelated to my son's addiction, and I have witnessed miracles in others who are now clean and sober.

Part of my work as a medical provider has been working in a residential treatment facility for homeless women in recovery from drugs and alcohol. We, the staff and I, sat at the staff meetings at times and just marveled at some of the women who were about to graduate after being there for two years.

We recalled the condition of these women at their admission to the program. They came to us homeless and destitute. Many had lost their rights as mothers, and had given up on themselves as human beings. They felt they no longer had meaning in their lives. By the time they graduated from the program, by the grace of God, they had reconnected to their Heavenly Father, and had been reminded of His love and forgiveness. He reminded them that He had not forgotten their names. We witnessed a pure miracle; transformation that could have only occurred as a result of God's grace and mercy! Praise God! It just proved to us, as a staff, that we were **not in control.** We wanted everyone of those ladies to make it, we did. God had other plans. Some of those ladies left with changed lives, some left prematurely due to stubbornness but saw the error of their ways and came back again, but some left, went back out to use again, and we never saw them again. But God definitely performed **miracles in lives** right before our eyes, and he did so regularly.

Sometimes even when our children have brief periods of recovery, we get to see miracles. Addiction can mean bouts of recovery and bouts of relapses. As a result, we may get short glimpses of sobriety from our loved ones and sometimes, even during those short glimpses there can be some miraculous healings that occur. So, don't miss those! I once saw a mother and daughter during the daughter's brief stint of sobriety get to make amends. This actually happened on the mother's death bed. It was priceless for her mother.

What I am saying here, is do not let your child's diagnosis of an addiction be a death sentence to your soul. God is always bigger than any challenge including addiction! That is where your healing and faith, as well as a closer walk with God and your prayer life, comes in.

Listen to the song: "Giants Fall" by Francesca Battistelli

*Amy Shirey PA C, LPC*

# 6

# BOUNDARIES

## Self-Protection

I hated the word boundaries. After years of therapy, I came to realize it was due to the fact that my mother said NO! to everything. God rest her soul. This very much stifled my sense of exploration and adventure, and it made me extremely anxious to venture out of my comfort zone. I realize now that it stemmed from her fear and anxiety and her need to control her surroundings. I have come to respect and appreciate the importance of boundaries. I now think about boundaries as a needed fence around your yard when there is a biting dog next door. Boundaries are meant to be for self-protection. When a child in your life gets trapped into his addiction and becomes toxic, he respects no boundaries. Because he is out of control, he will lie, steal, and run over you in every conceivable way.

At the age of about fourteen to seventeen, you still have some leverage with your child. However, your child with an addiction is usually very crafty at wearing you down and attempting to delude you into thinking you do not have any leverage or authority. He is usually very argumentative, manipulative, and can be downright abusive. If you are intimidated by him (whether female or male child) or you feel you are losing authority or all respect, that is a problem. Normally, these are the ages that teenagers are incrementally showing the ability to take on more responsibility. But when your child has an addiction, you began to wonder, "Where did my child go?" As a mother, instinctually, you often feel in your gut that something is wrong. Don't ignore that feeling in your gut. When you see or feel these warning signs, you have a problem! It leaves you feeling confused, dazed, and even makes you feel like you are going crazy, and of course blaming yourself. When your child is in early stages of addiction, you may begin to feel a significant struggle. As your child reaches the latter years of high school, it becomes palpable -- *if* the child makes it through high school. Because the child feels so angry at herself, she often lashes out at her parents. Usually on a deeper level, the child realizes she just can't get her life together. She regularly gets in trouble; she can't succeed either academically or socially; and she continually experiences negative consequences. However, the addictive disease in her keeps pushing her to continue to use drugs or alcohol or both, and that part of her just wants everyone to leave her alone. She often bullies, especially her mom. Why her mom? Because our children by instinct know moms are not abandoners.

## Take Action If Needed

Since this book is about healing *the* **gaping hole** of a parent's heart, IF you are being bullied, screamed at, blamed, or physically attacked by your child who you suspect is using or you know is using drugs or alcohol, STOP RIGHT NOW AND DO THESE TWO THINGS:

1. Immediately seek a Pastor, Christian Counselor, or Therapist experienced in Addiction and Codependency and Substance Abuse. MAKE AN APPOINTMENT.

2. Go immediately to Alanon. This is **essential** for a single parent! Addiction will absolutely defeat a single parent without a support system. This is harmful for YOU and your child!

## The Definition of Codependency

A Codependent is one (usually the parent) who has excessive emotional or psychological reliance on a partner (your loved one), typically a partner who requires support due to an illness or addiction.

In other words, your life has become so wrapped up in trying to rescue, fix, or save your child that you have totally lost your sense of self.

Listen to the song: "You Say" by Lauren Daigle.

*Amy Shirey PA C, LPC*

# 7

# A WORD ON ALANON

In this book, I am including many things that have helped and continue to help me with my sanity during the tortuous journey through my son's disease of addiction. <u>Alanon is an important one of them</u>. I was first introduced to the concept of Alanon while working in the hospital I mentioned. Alanon is for people who have a loved one with an addiction. It is based on the same "12-steps" approach as Alcoholics Anonymous (AA). I actually began attending out of desperation, and I was pleasantly surprised to find that it was an orderly, educational, and confidential program that was spiritually-based. At the time I started attending, I was in a complete fog. My life with my son had taken me down a dark path. He had already been arrested several times, and I was heartbroken, confused, and grieving.

## An Education

Alanon played an important role in my healing process; it educated me about boundaries in a positive manner. Since I came from a very dysfunctional family of origin, which by the way most of us do, boundaries represented extreme negativity to me. Everything was "no"; everything was "negative." But Alanon presented boundaries in a very healthy way, a way that I could hear and understand. Alanon helped me to see boundaries as a way to take care of myself and even a way to promote healthy relationships with others. This was especially true of my loved one with an addiction. It was an essential part of recovering from my pain.

## As A Support System

Alanon helps in numerous ways; it is also a support system in which you can talk confidentially to other moms who are dealing with the same situation as you. Some of these parents in Alanon have climbed out of the pit of despair, and they are there to help others who are still in the pit. Some who are attending have just realized they are in the pit. It is very difficult for people to understand what you are going through unless they have lived it. Counselors, family, and friends, who have not had children with addictions, can talk to you about your pain. But it is hard to understand the pain of having a child who has basically become a ghost of himself because of his addiction. Others in Alanon have experienced this and "get it." Alanon also helped me get to the point of being strong enough to say "no." All of this was reassuring to me.

## A Spiritual Program

Alanon is a spiritual program. Many in the program are Christians, but that is not a prerequisite. In Alanon, they urge you to take hold of a "Higher Power", but they do not define that "Higher Power." They allow the individual to choose her "Higher Power" for herself. However, in The Twelve Steps of Alanon, which they recite multiple times in the meetings, they do use the word God.

Alanon has helped many who have stopped attending church regain a relationship with God. The Eleventh Step of Alanon, AA, and Narcotics Anonymous (NA) encourages you to seek God through prayer and meditation, it allows you to define God as you understand Him. It also encourages you to pray for knowledge and power to carry out your God's will. So, Alanon encourages you to work on your relationship with God in a personal way through prayer and meditation!

## Loving your Loved One, Not the Addictive Disease

It is very important to realize that your child is not his addiction. Remember your child before she began to use, when she was six or seven years old? Maybe even ten or twelve? Even perhaps fourteen? Everyone is different. The beginning of substance abuse can start very early, but it does not always. I have worked with patients before that began their drug or alcohol abuse in their thirties or forties.

My point is this, as you watch your child self-destruct and continue to make horrible choices, Alanon will help you separate your loved one's addictive behavior from the person herself. Looking back and remembering your child before she was hijacked by the substances helps with this process. This is a *very delicate time-consuming process*, but it is crucial to separate the disease from the person deep inside.

As you encourage, guide, and coax him to turn from his destructive ways as mothers will do, you will be hurt as the disease takes hold. You will then likely become very angry; in fact, most of us become enraged. As mothers, we can even feel that we "hate our child" which leads to guilt and confusion. For me, separating the hate of the disease from the love of my child was like untangling a knotted necklace; I came to realize that what I hated was the disease that was destroying my child and my child's life, but I did not hate my child. Again, Alanon helped with this process.

Alanon educates parents to hate the disease and love their child and being able to talk about this concept in an environment that is supportive and understanding is where the extreme healing occurs. This is actually the same as what we are taught as Christians -- to love unconditionally your child who has an addictive disease.

I have helped many mothers who have said to me, and even to their loved ones with addiction, "I wish you would just go ahead and die!" Those without the experience of living with a loved one with addiction are aghast at this! Only the mother or parents with a child with a **gaping hole** in their heart can **get** this!! The pain is **so** intense in your heart **you feel** you cannot bear it!! **You** are dying inside watching your child suffer right in front of your eyes, but unlike watching your child die of cancer, you are watching your child participate in the self-destruction. Your anger and grief together are so excruciating it is overwhelmingly painful. Now, let's be careful not to judge here. This is so painful that mothers actually want to die as well. Here again is the great attribute of Alanon. There is no judgement in Alanon; they truly understand your emotional pain.

Even though you love your child with an addiction just like you would a loved one with cancer, leprosy, AIDS or any other chronic life-threatening illness, you still need boundaries, especially when he is actively using. Here is the tricky part about loving unconditionally a child with an addiction -- a loved one who is using may exhibit old behaviors of manipulation, stealing, and lying, which are not present with cancer, leprosy, and AIDS. As you can see, boundaries are essential.

While Stephen was in the grips of his addiction and would come to us for food or shelter, we had to make very hard choices. We almost always fed him unless he had income. If we fed him and he had income, he would use his money for drugs. Farther along in his addiction, I believe he was in his mid-twenties, we had to set the boundary that he could no longer live under our roof. We didn't trust him; he would steal our money to buy drugs or steal personal belongings like tools and sell them for drugs. So even though he was homeless, we had to turn him away. These decisions broke my heart. He had to stay in a local shelter, we had to change the locks on the door, get an alarm system and I hit my knees and sobbed in sorrow.

Now here is the hard part. How do you love your child but not enable his behavior? Again, Alanon helps with this, but prayer is crucial, and carefully, very carefully for me, it took a lot of practice and support from my Alanon sponsor, BUT most importantly a lot of prayer and direction from the Holy Spirit.

If I had not had my Loving Heavenly Father to sob to, I don't know where I would be today. God would often reassure me that He had my son in His care at those times. *I could feel His loving presence surround me.* His peace does pass all understanding. He does hear and wipe every tear. *I know it was because of the time I spent with Him that I could feel Him so close and dear to me in those troubled moments.* It does work, but you must do your part. You have to surrender and trust God.

## A Bit About Treatment

I want to insert a word about the treatment your loved one may need and the role you will play in that treatment. This is a frequent question that I get from mothers. I think it is an important one. As parents, we can spend an enormous amount of energy and money sending our loved ones to treatment facilities hoping that someone or some facility will be the next miracle. I certainly had some of these hopes. This can add to our exhaustion and disappointment. As I learned in Alanon, and as our loved ones learn in their twelve step spiritual programs, we must "keep it simple". While I believe my son got a lot from some of his treatments, some were probably my fruitless attempts to rescue him.

My son went to treatment about five times. Today, treatment received in some facilities is much too brief to provide the type of recovery needed for the addictions that are currently raking over our country. Based on a report from the National Institute on Drug Abuse (NIH Jan. 2019) every day more than 130 people in the United States die after overdosing on opioids. Long term treatment is essential for these addictions. **Long-Term Treatment** is desperately needed to adequately change and retrain brain chemistry for our loved ones abusing drugs.

There are long term treatment programs across our country. Sometimes they are as simple as half-way houses being organized by people who have long term recovery themselves and are trying to "give back." They take addicts and alcoholics in after detoxification, and put them on a rigid, structured schedule of twelve step meetings and work duty. They then add small home groups and use mentors who have been in recovery to sponsor them one on one. It works because it helps both sides of the fence, the newly recovering person and the person with long-term recovery who is doing the mentoring.

Look for one of these nonprofit agencies. But this is PARAMOUNT; agree to take your loved one to one of these facilities ONLY AFTER;

1. She agrees to detoxification. (which is medically necessary for alcohol, benzodiazepines and barbiturates) It usually only takes approximately ten days. There are free detox centers (at least in Georgia)

2. Your loved one comes to you and says, "I don't want this life anymore!" (of Addiction) Do not get caught up into forcing your loved one into treatment. It is a waste of your time, money, and energy. "Let Go and Let God" lead him to treatment. God knows better than you when and if your loved one is ready.

I share this treatment information with you because if you participate in taking your loved one to treatment AFTER she meets the conditions in #1 and #2, then you are being a "PART OF THE SOLUTION, NOT PART OF THE PROBLEM".

The alcoholic or addict goes to treatment an average three times. but not everyone who gets clean and sober goes to treatment! Some have gotten sober by just attending AA or NA and some say, "I got sober by the grace of God".

Listen to the song: "How Great is Your Love" by Phil Wickham

# 8

# A BIT MORE ABOUT ALANON

## A Foundation to Which You Can Always Return

You may find it interesting that in a Christian book, I am discussing Alanon. I believe that when you are struggling with your child having an addiction, you need *many* resources of support. There is usually an Alanon meeting everyday in most cities which means you can have the support of other mothers every day in person. It is not meant to take the place of your walk with your Heavenly Father, but rather it is to be used as an additional tool. Several self-care tools are needed when you have fallen into the pit of despair due to the **gaping hemorrhaging** hole in your heart that you experience when your child is on this destructive path. Alanon is a big one. You also need daily contact with your Heavenly Father, you need to eat nutritiously, and to get a good night's sleep. You also need to practice the Alanon concepts of healthy boundaries, and you need to let go of your loved one, and focus on letting God take care of him. These may sound like simple healthy ideas, but when you are exhausted it can honestly take you years to accomplish them. The important thing is to take it one step at a time and keep it simple.

## Keep Going Back, It Will Have Impact

As I mentioned, you are educated in Alanon about the behavioral traits of people with addictions, and this is vital as you are dealing with their behaviors. This is **so** necessary as you go through your life with your child, trying to make decisions about how to handle his demands. Our loved ones with addictions, while actively using, are full of manipulative, deceptive, behaviors. At first, we might be naïve to their crafty schemes, but eventually we catch on (even us moms). I don't know about you, but when my loved one was in his full manipulative, addictive, using behavior, it was hard sometimes not to "react" in anger. Alanon helped me to not be the "sick one" in the room. Alanon helped me to look at the dynamics of what was going on instead of taking it personally.

Think of Alanon as a college course with spiritual benefits. This education and the support you receive is a priceless foundation. Alanon's focus is to get you back on your feet, one meeting at a time. You cannot expect to go once, or twice, or even three times and be done. It is a process. It's like having to **retrain your brain**. It requires a change in your mind set to get healthy, especially if you have been in this whirlwind of dysfunction trying to rescue or fix your child for a long period of time. While your heart is breaking, your brain isn't necessarily working so well.

Alanon keeps it simple, guides your steps and encourages healthier decisions. Honestly, for some years you must allow the steps of Alanon and the support it offers to just sink in. Just allow yourself to sauté' in the concepts. Alanon's suggestions must become rote, routine, or like a reflex when you are dealing with your child who likely has a toxic brain and may be full of manipulative behaviors. Otherwise, you will fall back into old behaviors with your child-behaviors like neglecting your self-care and being too tired to stand up for yourself. This can lead you to fall back into allowing him to take advantage of you. And then, unfortunately, there you go again, "doing the old dance again," of codependent enabling and being a part of the problem, and not the solution. As my sponsor would tell me, "this old dance" is the same behavioral pattern that you and your addict or alcoholic have been doing that has kept the two of you sick for such a long time.

## Healing Recommendations

So Yes, go to Alanon and get a sponsor! Yes, get an education from Alanon! It not only educates you; it changes you and makes you **wiser** and that impacts **you** and it has a trickle-down effect that absolutely IMPACTS **your child**. When we live with an addict or alcoholic, we become very sick. Our Alanon sponsors often tell us that we are **as** sick as our loved one, or may have even been sick **before** that child was born! In other words, we may have had an alcoholic parent or even grandparent ourselves, which set us up to be an enabler. So, we have some work to do on ourselves, but we must also follow all of this with much heart felt prayer!

Now, if you have been working on yourself and doing a lot of the above steps, and you still feel like you absolutely cannot function, I want you to take this next chapter under serious consideration. This next chapter is basically about the medical diagnoses that can plague anyone but especially mothers and other family members with loved ones with addiction. So, reading and following the recommendations at the end of this chapter (Explanation of the Importance of Treatment) is an additional step that is sometimes necessary to get the intended healing God has for you.

But here is a special song for you first: "I Am Redeemed" by Big Daddy Weave

*Amy Shirey PA C, LPC*

# 9

# DEPRESSION, ANXIETY, ANGER, AND PTSD

A mother with a child with addiction can be overwhelmed with sadness, anger, fatigue, and fear. The sadness along with the realization that her child has a lifelong disease, can certainly be very emotionally difficult. I remember telling my son, "I wish it was me with the disease of addiction, not you." God did not plan it that way, but I wanted to take it from him. I wanted to be the one that had to deal with the day by day pain. I wanted to deal with the shame he was feeling and the torturous battle to stay clean. Of course, in my limited mind since I had not experienced how hard it is to stay clean, I imagined I could do it. But who knows how hard it is until you walk in those shoes? It must be very, very, difficult, look how many die from this disease. Have mercy. Just as Christ had mercy.

**The Symptoms of Each**

Sometimes, the sadness of having a child with an addictive disease can lead one into a deep depression. If you have a history of depression, or a history of abuse of any kind, especially if you have never had any previous healing or treatment, you are certainly at risk to develop clinical depression. Some mothers of loved ones with an addictive disease may have anxiety disorders. The good news is that there is healing and treatment FOR BOTH! I want you to be clear here, of the symptoms of Depression and of Anxiety. These two disorders go "hand in hand" because they are very much related in terms of brain chemistry.

If you are experiencing **symptoms of major depression** such as:

Feeling depressed mood most of the day, nearly every day for a two-week period of time or more

Or; have markedly diminished interest in all activities most of the day nearly every day, or most all activities most of the day nearly every day.

This can be by subjective report (feeling sad or empty) or by observation made by others (appears tearful)

Plus; 3 or more of these:

Have significant weight loss, when not dieting, or weight gain (a change of more than 5% of body weight in a month) or decrease or increase in appetite nearly every day.

Have Insomnia or hypersomnia (sleeping too much) nearly every day

If you are experiencing restlessness, or lethargy nearly every day, (observable by others not merely subjectively, feeling of restlessness or being slowed down)

Fatigue, or loss of energy nearly every day,

Feelings of worthlessness, excessive or inappropriate quilt, nearly every day, or

Diminished ability to think or concentrate, and or indecisiveness, nearly every day, (either subjectively or observed by others)

If you are having recurrent thoughts of death, (not just fear of dying), recurrent suicidal ideations, without a specific plan or a suicide attempt or a specific plan for committing suicide

Go directly to the end of this chapter and read "**Explanation of Treatment**" and follow the recommendations! OR if you are having **Anxiety Symptoms:**

Anxiety can occur with or without Panic Disorder

(I include Panic Disorder because often my patients, mothers of addicts have panic, Panic disorder and anxiety often go "hand in hand with depression")

## Anxiety Symptoms:

- Excessive anxiety and worry with apprehensive expectation occurring more days than not, for at least 6 months

- Excessive worry that you or your loved one is going to die
- Finding it difficult to control the worry
- Restlessness or feeling keyed up or on edge
- Being easily fatigued
- Difficulty concentrating or mind going blank
- Irritability
- Muscle tension
- Sleep disturbances (difficulty falling or staying asleep, or restless unsatisfying sleep)

## Panic Disorder Symptoms:

- Panic attacks; which are experienced with, some or all of the following,
- Pounding heart or accelerated heart rate (palpitations)
- Sweating
- Trembling or shaking
- Sensations of shortness of breath or smothering
- Feeling of choking
- Chest pain or discomfort
- Nausea or abdominal distress
- Feeling dizzy, unsteady, lightheaded, or faint
- Derealization (feelings as if you are not present in the room, a sort of "unreality feeling") also called depersonalization and described as being detached from oneself.
- Fear of losing control or going crazy
- Fear of dying
- Paresthesias (numbness or tingling sensations)
- Chills or hot flushes

Panic attacks can occur with or without agoraphobia. Agoraphobia is a Latin word that means fear of enlarged spaces. In other words, some people with panic, feel the need to be enclosed. A person with panic may feel they want to stay at home, and cannot tolerate going places like the grocery store or any other large department stores. Basically, the anxiety makes them too insecure, and the close quarters makes them feel more secure.

Again, if you are suffering with any of the above Anxiety Symptoms with or without Panic Attacks and/or Agoraphobia go directly to "**Explanation of Treatment**" at the end of this chapter for recommendations.

Ok, now what if all you feel is anger? There *are* some parents whose primary complaint is just feeling angry, really angry. Sometimes I have had parents ask me, "Why do I just feel angry all the time when other parents are sad, depressed or say they just feel like nervous wrecks?" It is as though they think there is something wrong with their response. They think feeling depressed or anxious is the *only* "appropriate response," instead of anger.

My husband would often say, "We didn't have a single child who left the nest naturally." He was so right. Due to the fact that we had a blended family, and an addict in the family, our children without an addiction reached late adolescence and early adulthood, and scattered. But when you have an addict in the family, *they* may hover and stay as long as they can, and try to mooch off their family members hoping their family members will enable them. As a result of their lengthy stay and the chaos, associated with the addict, you as a parent are often privy to a lot of traumatic experiences such as arrests, incarcerations, car wrecks, hospitalizations, overdoses, court appearances, the list can be exhaustive. These experiences can "clip" parents at their knees and knock them off their feet just when they least expect it, leaving them feeling traumatized. Which leads to the last subtitle of this Chapter: Post Traumatic Stress Disorder (PTSD).

Some family members with loved ones with addiction suffer with PTSD. **ANGER** is one of the predominant symptoms of PTSD.

With PTSD there is pure exhaustion physically, emotionally, mentally, and financially. When you add to this the regular routine of life experiences, it feels as if you are carrying a ton of bricks around your neck. It seems you are always fearful that the next "terrible thing is going to happen". Life with an addict in the home is full of chaos, confusion, and uncertainty. The **disease is in control** and the **addict is swirling out of control**. For the addict, impulse takes over, and there is lawlessness, stealing, and lying, and that often means danger. Nothing is beyond happening, if it will score the addict his next fix or high. For the mother with the **gaping hole** in her heart this adds "terror" and sometimes anger. These years of terror, anger, and fear produce the symptoms of PTSD.

## Symptoms of PTSD

A person with PTSD experienced, witnessed or was confronted with an event or events that involved actual or *threatened* death or serious injury or *a threat* to the physical integrity of self or others. The person's response involved intense fear, helplessness, or horror.

If you have experienced any of these symptoms, you likely have some degree of PTSD:

- Recurrent distressing dreams of your child using or getting high

- Intense psychological distress at exposure of your child being high or using

- Persistent avoidance of thoughts, feelings or conversations associated with your child's using

- Inability to recall important aspects of your child's history of drug/alcohol use (It all runs together after a while)

- Marked diminished interest in participation in significant activities
- Feeling of detachment or estrangement from others (desire to isolate socially)
- Restricted range of affect (e.g. unable to have loving feelings)
- Persistent symptoms of increased arousal
- Difficulty falling or staying asleep
- Irritability or outburst of **anger**
- Difficulty concentrating
- Hypervigilance
- Exaggerated startle response

## The Explanation of The Importance of Treatment

**Do not hesitate** to seek medical attention for **any** of these symptoms. If you have symptoms of Depression, Anxiety with or without Panic, with or without Agoraphobia, or symptoms of PTSD, either a Family Practitioner with a Physician Assistant experienced in mental health or a Psychiatrist should be completely qualified to treat these symptoms with non-addictive medications.

**If you are having suicidal thoughts or thoughts of wanting to hurt yourself or others** go ahead and pick up the phone and call 911 for help. You must get help for yourself. Chances are you are exhausted and depleted in terms of brain chemistry-this is fixable. Healing is often a multifaceted approach. First things first! Let's get you stable enough brain chemistry wise to be able to absorb the healing you deserve. God has put this book in your hands for a reason. Making that call is the first step toward healing and God WILL carry you through.

## A Prescription for All

I always told my patients who were hesitant to take medications, "You know, God created the human beings that invented these medications and those who prescribe these medications to help us." There are approximately a dozen different brands of non-addictive antidepressants and anti-anxiety medications. You and your Practitioner will have to choose the medication that will work best for you. Quite honestly, sometimes you many even have to try one or two before you find the correct one for you. This is no different than finding the right blood pressure medication that works best for your body, however; *THESE MEDICATIONS WORK BEST ONLY IF YOU USE THEM WITH PRAYER, AND ASK GOD TO BLESS THEM!"*

If the loved one with an addiction gets help in the form of detoxification and a spiritually based long-term treatment program and the family gets educational support through Alanon, and commits to a strong spiritual walk with God, the years of anguish and torture that families have endured can be obliterated by the love of our Savior Jesus Christ.

*Amy Shirey PA C, LPC*

# 10

# STEPHEN'S FIRST TREATMENT

## Tough Calls

When Stephen was about nineteen years old, he was still living at home. He was a sophomore in the local college, although he had barely passed his freshman year. I was working full time and he was really slacking with his college classes. I knew in my heart of hearts that he wasn't applying himself and blew me off whenever I asked about his grades. I would come home from work and he would be on the couch playing video games. He looked to me that he had perhaps been using. He looked sluggish, and seemed to have no motivation. He was not interested in his surroundings like his room or his hygiene, and was not interested in interacting with any of the family members. I thought the semester would never end. He would give me elusive excuses about his course work and grades. I suspected he was not doing well but a mother hopes against hope. Doesn't she? He failed two of three courses and I confronted him. I also found pills in his bedroom.

Steve and I told him he had to either go into treatment, or leave our home. He proceeded to tell me I was crazy, and that I was not going to throw him out. I replied, "Don't make me call the police. We are going out to eat, be gone when we return." Now... About that **gaping hole** in a mother's heart. Your adult child is nineteen years old, and you have just put him out on the street for the first time, definitely not a good feeling. He has no money, no job, and you have just found pills in his jeans. I honestly did know he had a girl that he had been seeing, with an apartment, but I also knew she was a waitress, so that wasn't going to be a long-term arrangement due to financial constraints. My son returned home about eight months later saying he wanted to come home and straighten out his life, so he agreed to treatment for the first time. But as a mother, those months were agonizing. I was filled with fear and the anxiety was gripping. Although I was attending Alanon, I had a long way to go to get any peace. My son was only beginning his journey. He went to treatment for likely all the wrong reasons, but it planted some seeds.

## Planting Seeds

I don't believe any treatment is wasted. My son is now thirty-two years old and still talks about his treatment he received at nineteen. His brain was not as totally toxic at nineteen, and I believe he received some very vital basics at his first treatment program. He was there for six months and upon returning home, returned to college and relapsed approximately six to eight months later, but I still believe it was helpful.

He learned things such as, his addiction is a genetic disease, that he must abstain from all addictive chemicals, not just the ones he was using at the time. He was introduced to The Twelve Steps of AA and NA and the need to change his playmates (people he was using drugs with) and playgrounds (places he was going and doing drugs). He was also taught about sponsorship. All these tenets are still used and relative in recovery circles today.

The most important aspect of this experience was that while I had just begun attending Alanon, it helped me to take this hard stand (treatment vs find another place to live). It was exactly what he needed even though it was not easy. It was a very difficult decision for Steve and me, but our son, as a result of his addictive behaviors, had started taking advantage of us by taking extra change and money out of my purse, not attending college which we were paying for, not being honest with us, and actually lying about his grades. He was in his second year of college so to allow this behavior in our home to continue would have been enabling. Did I say this was a very hard decision on a mother's heart?

If I am totally honest, which I will continue to be in this entire book, I think at this point I was acting out of fear because as a health care professional I knew, really knew, the horrors of addiction. Also, even though this would be considered by some to be early stage addiction, since he was nineteen, and at this point, he was likely only using marijuana and occasional Adderall, I could feel him falling deeper and deeper into substance abuse. With my son's heavy family history, and him experiencing recurrent negative consequences due to substance abuse, I knew in my gut he had an addiction.

## Learning to Embrace Their Treatment

Eventually mothers can feel a relief when their loved ones are in treatment. Think about it, they are tucked in snuggly at night, we know where they are, who they are with, and what they are doing. They are not on the streets and are not using. The people who are caring for them have their best interest at heart. Be smart, if your loved one calls you and gives you a line, wanting you to check them out of treatment, or get them out of jail, don't buy it. They are most likely just craving and having second thoughts about being in treatment and wanting to get out so they can use. Particularly if it hasn't been at least two to three months-the time it takes for them to get some clarity of mind. Try to relax while your loved one is there. Even if they are incarcerated. As difficult as that can be, if you leave them in jail, you will gradually see a change in their attitude as the drugs or alcohol get out of their system. Initially, they may call and plead for you to get them out or send them money but over time, they typically mellow and begin to realize that they are responsible for being there.

Take this time to self-care. If they are in jail and ringing your phone off the hook, don't answer the phone. I know that is difficult but in the first two to three weeks communication is fruitless because your loved one's brain is toxic and he is still full of manipulative ploys and blame. Many loved ones with addiction have had epiphanies while in jail and being in jail can be safer than being on the streets. Thankfully, if he is in treatment he will not be allowed to call. Regardless of his location, jail or treatment, he will soon be out and that in itself will present a different set of concerns, so enjoy your break.

Oh boy, do we get nervous when they get discharged, even if they did well in a treatment program and stayed the allotted time. This is why we have to have our support system and more importantly our close walk with our Heavenly Father. I was clueless that I had many years, eighteen to be exact, of trials to face after Stephen's first treatment. I was also clueless and thought his disease would be fixed by treatment in a facility. God had prepared a journey for me, He showed me that treatment programs are often a starting point because they educate. I had a lot to learn ahead.

Listen to: "Maybe It's Ok" by We Are Messengers

# 11

# ADDICTION IN THE FAMILY OF ORIGIN

**Changing Patterns**

Neither of my parents drank or did drugs, however my paternal grandfather was a heavy drinker. As a result, the patterns of a dysfunctional family system were imbedded in my parents. These patterns were; don't talk about your problems, don't trust your feelings or anyone else, and don't allow yourself to feel your feelings. This was a very stoic, sterile, environment, typical in the 1950's. These patterns *can* be passed down generation to generation without even realizing it. They can even have an impact on your spiritual life. Think about it. If you have lived in a family for eighteen years without feeling that you can talk about anything that is bothering you, you may not feel that you can even talk to God about it.

If you are never allowed in your family of origin to feel your feelings, and you have not felt you could even share them with your Heavenly Father; then, you are likely stuffed with feelings, even pain, about your child with an addiction. Well, God created us with the ability to feel feelings, right? He gave us the feeling of sadness, anger, and joy just to name a few. I don't think He then planned for us to never feel those buggers! No! The Bible is full of examples of people with feelings. Even Jesus got angry! And then there is the Bible verse about making a joyful noise to our Lord!

*Make a joyful noise unto the Lord, all the earth: make a loud noise, and rejoice, and sing praise Sing unto the Lord with the harp; with the harp, and the voice of a psalm. With trumpets and sound of cornet make a joyful noise before the Lord, the King. (Psalm 98:4-6 KJV)*

## Self-Care

So... go to Alanon and Christian counseling to learn healthy ways of dealing with your feelings and how to trust them. Go for your child, and do it for yourself! If you are expecting your loved one with an addiction to do what she needs to do to get healthy, clean, and sober then what about you? What do you need to do to get healthy? Dealing with our deep stuffed unresolved feelings is part of healing and getting healthy. Through sharing these feeling in Counseling and with your Heavenly Father a healing process begins.

If your child does get into a recovery program, most programs require him to attend twelve step meetings. They also often request and encourage strongly that the family members go to Alanon. Get yourself to a meeting! If you don't feel comfortable at the first meeting you try, go to another one in a different part of the city. It is like finding the right church. Give it time, and **full** effort. Find yourself a good Christian counselor who understands addictive disease and codependency (codependency-excessive emotional/psychological reliance on a partner with illness/addiction).

Think about it. You have been interacting with your loved one in a certain way, for X number of years, since he began his addictive behavior, and for some, that may have even been before he was deep into substances. Remember my son at fifteen, and the policeman's comment? So how long do you think it takes to reprogram your brain to change your behavior? Most experts and professionals recommend attending Alanon for life. I certainly see the merit in this. Alanon strongly encourages you to stop obsessing about your addict because that is not only a distraction from your spirituality and healing, but obsessing will make you sick AND will harm you loved one.

You have a responsibility to yourself to take this prescription:

**Yes!** Do Christian therapy to help nurture yourself.

**Yes!** Absolutely go to Alanon consistently.

And, **if** you have clinical symptoms of depression or anxiety, and are having trouble functioning, then, **Yes**, take a non-addictive antidepressant or anti-anxiety medication under the care of a physician. But most IMPORTANTLY and ESSENTIALLY: GET DOWN ON YOUR KNEES BEFORE GOD!

Listen to the song: "The Well" by Casting Crowns

*Amy Shirey PA C, LPC*

# 12

# HE WILL LEAD YOU TO HEALING

### Surviving ICU

Think of what you would do to survive if you had a deadly illness and you were in the hospital in ICU. **You would fight for your life, and pray to God to save you.** *This is no different.* Actually, when we are over our heads in codependency, we get so sick it can actually make us physically ill and we may eventually end up in ICU. Numerous mothers of loved ones with addiction that I have treated had multiple health issues. This was often due to pure neglect of their health. They were so wrapped up and obsessed in their addict's life that they totally ignored their own health issues. Many would be overweight with high blood pressure, diabetes, or thyroid issues, and had not even seen their family physician in years. They would offer a hand full of excuses as to why they had not seen their physician, mostly related to the fact that they were too busy "taking care" of their loved one with an addiction.

Have you ever heard what the stewardess says on a commercial airplane? She instructs the passengers, "If the plane goes down, parents are to put their oxygen mask on first, so that they might not pass out and can assist their children." That is exactly what applies here. If you do not self-care, not only are you no help to your child with an addiction, you are not helping yourself.

So, as I alluded to earlier, Alanon is a starting point to get you out of ICU. It is difficult in words to sum up the benefits you will receive from attending the self-care program of Alanon. It is akin to telling someone about a magnificent movie, of all time. It is an experience. *You will get out of it, what you put into it.* It is your personal experience. I had an elderly Christian sponsor early on in Alanon, who has passed on. She was so full of wisdom and humor, just to sit in her presence was a joy. She was so good at one-liners, "Hands off, pays off," "Remember, you didn't cause it, you can't control it, and you can't cure it!", "Don't do for him, what he can do for himself" and about Alanon, she would say, "If you don't feel like going to a meeting, you better run to one." All of these wise words and many others helped retrain my brain. I believe Alanon, and the spiritual aspect of it, played a vital role in leading me back to my knees which led me face down before my Lord, and this is where I received the peace I have today, this is what led to my surrender.

Well let me stop here and say … I have given you a lot of good ideas about Alanon which offers excellent education and coping skills. But I want to share with you what I realized. The **MISSING KEY** to survive your child's addiction is YOUR RELATIONSHIP WITH GOD. This is going to be the vital sustaining **HEALTH** component of your life. This is the **Missing Key** that so many mothers do not pursue, thus they never get the peace that they need. Even Alanon points you in that direction, because living with a child with an addiction is gut wrenching at best. Over my life my spiritual walk has matured, but what happened next absolutely brought me down to my face before God. How did I get to this point of desperation?

My son had been into his addiction for about ten years, he was about twenty-five years old at this point. My husband and I had been regular Alanon attenders, and pretty much had the concepts of The Twelve Steps of Alanon down. What was missing in my life, was a deep faith and belief that God loved me enough to SAVE me from this torture. Huh? Wait a minute. Save me? I had been working tirelessly for ten years for my son to be saved, and honestly it wasn't working. Actually, his addictive disease had progressed! He was extremely sick. He had lost an enormous amount of weight, he had dark circles under his eyes, and he looked like the walking dead. It was heart breaking to see him. Honestly, I just couldn't seem to let go of him completely and consistently. I kept continuing to justify holding on, and kept telling myself that I felt as a parent, on some level, I could not abandon him because he was so sick. I felt he was my responsibility, even though I knew he was moving into adulthood. But if I am totally truthful, I could not let go of him, due to **my** need of not wanting to lose him. At this point, my sponsor's comment "I need Alanon and church," changed my life.

## Is Alanon Enough?

I grew up in a Southern Baptist church. At about the age of nine or ten, I felt the Holy Spirt touch my heart and tell me to go, and make public, my love for my Savior Jesus. At that point, Jesus came into my heart for life. I truly felt God pulled me out of an abyss that day. My home life was very rigid and depressing and oppressive. I was a very sad, depressed, little girl, but I believed in the love of Jesus. I believed then, and believe to this day, that Jesus was telling me He was there for me, even though my childhood was difficult and filled with verbal and emotional abuse.

As an adult, I continued to grow as a Christian sometimes doing better than others, and definitely straying during my adult life at times. I certainly strayed and lost faith after a divorce, but my son's addiction made my faith almost nonexistent. I could not understand how God could allow this to happen to my son. So, I had really stopped attending church and felt my prayers had gone unanswered.

At the peak of my son's drug use, God led me to a young church. I had grown up in a Southern Baptist church during the late 50's and early 60's when typically, much of the focus was on doing the "right thing", or "bad things" would happen to you (perhaps that was my mother's rendition). As my son was self-destructing and my despair was discernible, I was looking for something different. God knew I needed healing, and the church He led me to was a very healing environment. This turned out to be very helpful at this point in my life. I was hurting, really hurting. I had a **gaping, hemorrhaging, hole** in my heart.

I could hardly function. I needed to feel God's love, and I believe God led me to just the right place. My husband and I began attending this very small non-denominational church. They put a lot of focus on healing. I believe God led me specifically there, at that season of my life, because I would often sob during the service, and the Pastor would kindly say, "Just let it go sister, release all that pain, lay it at the feet of Jesus." And so, I did, and it began... My relationship with my Savior became more real, more tangible, more personal. I allowed myself to be vulnerable with God. I began to ask Jesus to help me through my day, even for little things. I remember asking him to help me see my next patient, help me get up out of the bed and get dressed. I even asked him to help me get out of the car and carry my belongings into the building. I was distressed and exhausted at that point in my life, but Jesus was right there helping me every step of the way. He will do the same for you. I read my Jesus is Calling (Sarah Young) meditation book daily. I did anything I could do to feel closer to God. I listened daily to Christian praise music, it calmed and encouraged me.

## What More Can You Do?

Without this deep visceral crying out to God, I truly do not believe I would be where I am today. I came to Him with all my pain in the most vulnerable way, holding nothing back. There is nothing that will bring a mother to her knees faster than not being able to find her child on the streets while he is out using drugs, or when her child is being arrested and going to jail or prison. The answer is God. He knows your pain. He has sacrificed HIS SON. He will carry you through. All you have to do is turn to HIM and put your burdens at His feet.

Listen to: "Rescue" by Lauren Daigle

# 13

# MY SON WENT TO PRISON...

## The Stress

There are times you feel you are not going to make it.

At the same time my husband and I were dealing with Stephen in the grips of his addiction on a self-destructive path, my eighty-nine-year-old father was living with us, and of course needed my attention. I had a full time Counseling private practice, with patients that needed me, and I was also working as a consulting Physician Assistant at a residential treatment facility for homeless women in recovery who required weekly evaluation for medical and psychiatric needs. Consequently, I was emotionally drained, and tired of being pulled in several directions, and in addition, in the back of my mind, I worried that my son might go to jail, prison, or overdose and die. My situation was not unique. Many mothers have just as much stress on their plate, and want to give in and give up.

Complicating this scenario, is that as mothers we know we have no control. We have no control over the destiny of our child, or our adult child, as he heads down this dangerous path. I could acknowledge that he had a choice. I had to decide to trust in God, and hand my child over to Him. I remember asking God, "You mean be OK with the fact that it may be part of YOUR plan for Stephen to die, or go to jail or prison?" My precious Heavenly Father answered me, "Stephen's life is not your call."

## The Loss

Whoa! That was hard to hear, so I decided to ask again right? Isn't that what you would do? I said, "God that would break my heart, it would kill me to have to feel that sadness, or to have to bury my child, or to even have to visit him in prison for the rest of his life. I don't think I could bear it if something horrific happened to him." God said to me, "So beloved, you are going to spend the rest of your life living in fear of that which I may not have commanded to happen? Where is your faith that I have positive plans and a positive future for Stephen? Can you not visualize that? Can you not even imagine that?" I hit my knees in prayer for forgiveness for my lack of faith and gave thanks. "Yes! Father, forgive me for losing faith and thank you Lord in advance for the blessing that you are going to bestow on my son! I will claim those blessings! Amen!"

I realized what I needed to do, day by day. I needed to get out of the way of Stephen's and God's journey. Yes, I needed to protect my home with boundaries. Logistically, this meant locking up money, checkbooks, medications, and other valuables. I needed to tell my son, once again, that he needed to find another place to live since he was not, once again, doing what he needed to do to stay sober. But most importantly, in addition to enjoying my elderly father and my husband, I began fervently focusing on my relationship with God. My commitment was to build stronger my trust and intimacy with my Heavenly Father and sit still and concentrate on His love for me, and His promises of caring for me and His children.

## The Pain

One month later, my son was arrested. Funny how things work! This arrest led to prison, to prison in his twenties. He had to spend two of his next birthdays, Christmases, and Thanksgivings in prison. When I found out in the courtroom, my body felt heavy. It felt like a dream. I kind of went into a trance when the judge said the sentence. It felt like someone had died. I could not fathom not touching my son for what I thought at the time would be perhaps five years.

I can't imagine how mothers that have to endure longer sentences survive. I am an affectionate mother. I have always given hugs. I used to rub his back, his feet, his head, when he was young. Even when he was a baby, I delighted in his soul and spirit. I hold those experiences as very special memories. I played with him as a child on the beach, cuddling in my bed, holding him as a two-year-old, breastfeeding him as an infant as he gazed up at me, telling him God loves you, Mom loves you. I have loved him dearly. I breathed in his innocence; I provided a safe haven for him to explore. We have laughed and cried together, and yet somewhere I lost sight of him, and he lost sight of himself. He had been such a joyful child until the disease of addiction took him away from me, and away from himself. Some say there is no greater love than the love of a mother and her child. We breathe in our child's soul. We are forever connected by that invisible umbilical cord so we feel their pain.

However, I have learned and have come to believe that at some point as they achieve adulthood, we must let go. We must surrender and allow them to experience their own pain, so they can grow. Their pain is between them and God. Each of us as individuals decide whether to connect to God with our pain, or try to deal with it ourselves. What will we choose? Will we turn to Him with our pain, or turn away from Him and deal with it on our own? That decision can begin our dependency on our Heavenly Father if we choose it, and this is the place that miracles happen. We must not interfere with this process in our child. I realized that my son needed to depend on God, not me.

Now back to the gaping hole of a mother's heart. I was standing in the courtroom. I had never been arrested in my life. I had just paid an attorney $1500.00 and he tried to get ME to pitch a spiel to the judge about a treatment facility (since I have a medical degree), and the judge basically shut me up, and said to my son, "You are a thug and a piece of s___! Eight years serve three!" I went into sort of a trance. Stephen was in his early twenties. I turned to my husband and said, "What did he say?" I was in shock and the weeks and months that followed were terrifying and traumatic.

Trauma is often a part of the experience of mothers with children with addictions. The trauma can result from incarcerations, shootings, vehicular accidents, the list goes on. All the more reason we need the healing balm of the Lord Jesus in order to recover from all the wounds of our hemorrhaging heart.

Let me stop here and say, when we experience these traumatic events our shame often resurfaces. I could not even imagine jail, much less prison. I grew up in a middle-class family. My parents were elementary school teachers who spanked my sister and me even if we had to stay after school for "misbehaving." My parents were Christians, and taught my sister and me to follow the law (May my mother and father rest in peace). Thank the good Lord they didn't have to deal with either of their daughters having an addiction! But even with all my understanding of addiction, it was very difficult to utter the words… "My son is in prison." I definitely felt shame.

I have spoken to many mothers whose children have been involved in drug crimes of stealing or even violent crimes related to drugs, and they were mortified and yet somehow felt responsible and ashamed for their child's behavior. I am here to tell you that God has His arms open wide to hold you mothers in your pain!

**The System**

I remember getting one of the first letters my son sent me from prison. He had been sent from the local jail to Jackson State Prison. All inmates from Georgia go there first for an initial evaluation. They are there a couple of months until they are placed in a different prison where they remain, or they are moved around to different prisons.

While in Jackson State Prison, Stephen was placed in a cell with an inmate who had been charged with murder three previous times, and this time convicted. You can imagine as a mother of a son in his twenties how one would not sleep that night and the nights that followed. Your heart goes straight to terror. His letters were tense and anxious, asking me to stay on top of his parole board for his temporary parole month (TPM) fearful that a mistake would be made and he would have to stay longer than his allotted time. It was obvious he was also very fearful and distrustful.

While in prison, in his letters he talked of the tasteless food and how little they fed them, the weight he could not gain, the total lack of privacy, and how much he missed seeing the sunshine. He was constantly requesting that I send him books, he read voraciously, likely to avoid the time dragging. It was expensive, and exhaustive and very scary for me. Sending money for an inmate is a scam, so not only is your loved one in a horrendous environment, but as his mother you are paying ridiculous fees to send your loved one extra food, toiletries, socks, stamps, or anything such as this. His endless requests on top of my grief and overwhelming sadness, felt like I was drowning but at the same time, I could sense his anxiety and fear so I felt an intense need to respond to his letters.

It was very difficult to find the right words to say what I was feeling at the time my son was sentenced to prison. I felt numb, sad, grief stricken, lost. In my mind I was saying, "Well at least he is not dead," or "This may very well be the miracle you have been praying for." But in my heart, I was well feeling a **gaping hole**, **a hemorrhaging** heart. "Never mind," I thought, "You do have a right to feel this emotional pain." But at that moment, in the beginning, I could feel nothing, I was in total shock!

To Stephen's credit, he would never tell me the specifics of the dangerous situations he encountered in prison. He spared me those parts. I truly believe he knows a mother's heart could not bear to hear that part. I'm just thankful to God that He protected my son. I diligently prayed for my son's safety. I prayed for Warrior Angels to surround him and asked that:

*No weapon forged against you will prevail, and you will refute every tongue that accuses you. This is the heritage of*

**the servants of the Lord, and this is their vindication from me, declares the Lord. (Isaiah 54:17 NIV)**

On my knees, literally on my knees in tears, I pleaded that God please keep him safe.

## My God

I also hit my knees and asked God to let me feel His presence. I asked Him to let me feel the **angels** He had sent to me and anything else that would help me to excavate the pain, to vomit it up, to spit it out, breathe it out, and for the blood of Jesus to cover my broken bleeding heart. I asked God to cover my pain with His loving balm, to help me to recognize that I was hurting and to help me to realize it's ok to feel sad and scared. I kept thinking of Jesus's mother Mary and how terrible it must have been for her to watch what Jesus went through, what torture she endured!

I knew I would get through this experience because of God's love, even though at the time, I was experiencing excruciating emotional pain. I had to learn to love myself because I knew God loved me, and treat myself with tenderness and kindness because I knew that was what God wanted me to do. I asked God to help me to listen to my soul and discern what my heart and soul were experiencing, and I asked that the Holy Spirit would give me guidance as to what I should do to help myself.

I began to realize that I needed to let go and let God heal me. I needed to pray, worship, and read my Bible. I was always such a hard nose about "doing" my part. Right then, all I could do was sit and be still. That's all I could do, and maybe that was exactly what I needed to do and where I needed to be. So, I took that time and sat still, to be present with God's loving touch and magnificence.

Also, at that time in my life, I had lost my mother and father both of whom lived with my husband and me. We had cared for them up to their deaths. I was also running my own Counseling private practice. The stress was over the top. My husband's company had gone under due to the "Great Recession" and he was in mid-life having to look for a job. Our other son was also laid off from his job due to the economy, and was looking for employment. His wife, thank God, was working, but they had a small child. I believe all of these circumstances culminated at the same time and precipitated my fall, my fall on my face before the Lord.

It is unbelievable how much turmoil you can experience in your soul, when you know, or have a foreboding fear, that your child or adult child is in danger for his life. Without faith in God, there is no way to survive this torture of your soul. Getting down on your knees and in my case on my face before God, will save your life.

Throughout the whole prison experience, I was so angry! Over and over, I felt disappointed and fearful, and I felt despair. I was fighting to handle this extreme stress on my own, but **God never left my side**! He absolutely carried me even when I screamed, and sobbed, and cried, and yelled. I was often my own worst enemy, forcing myself to push on, and push hard, to partially block the pain, in spite of extreme fatigue, both physical and mental. I was told by a physician that I had Fibromyalgia. It was excruciating. I had poured every ounce of myself into being a mom to Stephen, and now, I was paying the price.

No, I couldn't conceive of saying to my son, "Well you made your bed so sleep in it!", or "You are grown, and in prison with a lot of evil adult men who have committed violent crimes so learn from it!" I wasn't there yet, and I didn't know if I ever would be. My ONLY recourse was to turn to my Lord and Savior Jesus Christ.

## Collapsing in God's Arms

So, while my son was in prison, in the state evaluation facility with the general criminal population for selling opioid pills and while he had been placed in a cell with someone charged with murder, my heart felt like it had a **gaping hole hemorrhaging blood.** For me at this point, surrendering to God was more like collapsing into God's arms.

Many of you mothers may be at this same point. You **can** collapse in God's arms. He **will** catch you. This is the beginning of the journey. The collapse is just the start. Don't stop there. Continue to work on the relationship. The relationship with God is what brings the change in you, which is life changing.

So, I collapsed, and for twenty-two months, which is the time my son actually ended up serving in prison, (thank God not five or eight years), I prayed daily for his safety. I also asked for the Holy Spirit to help me put on "The Armor of God" (Ephesians 6: 10-17) to protect me from the lies told to me and the lies told to me by myself, of all the horrors you hear of prison hood.

*Finally, be strong in the Lord and in his mighty power. Put on the full armor of God, so that you can take your stand against the devil's schemes. For our struggle is not against flesh and blood, but against the rulers, against the authorities, against the powers of this dark world and against the spiritual forces of evil in the heavenly realms. Therefore, put on the full armor of God, so that when the day of evil comes, you may be able to stand your ground, and after you have done everything, to stand. Stand firm then, with the belt of truth buckled around your waist, with the breastplate of righteousness in place, and with your feet fitted with the readiness that comes from the gospel of peace. In addition to all this, take up the shield of faith, with which you can extinguish all the flaming arrows of the evil one. Take the helmet of salvation and the sword of the Spirit, which is the word of God. (Ephesians 6:10-17 NIV)*

But honestly at first…as I told you, I fell to the floor, face down, at the feet of Jesus and pleaded for Jesus to help me and my son. It was the lowest point in my life. How could my son, my boy, go to prison?

Listen to the song: "Gracefully Broken" by Matt Redman (feat. Tasha Cobbs)

When I finally laid my eyes on my son, when he came home, he was pale, malnourished, and underweight. He also came home extremely anxious, with difficulty sleeping, and an inability to talk about being in prison. It took him a long time to feel better physically, mentally, and emotionally. He has spoken of the fact that you have to develop ways to cope in prison to survive. The only one he shared, was that he befriended the Hispanic community who he explained "really stuck together" and he came out of prison basically bilingual. He would not allow me to visit him while in prison and finally broke down and told me that the inmates would fornicate in the visitation room in full site and he did not want me exposed to that during family visits. He spoke of the gangs and the yelling and the need to sleep with "one eye open" and the games people played. He tried to stay on work detail as much as he possibly could so he would be gone during the day. Honestly, I do not know how he survived.

I share this prison scenario for one reason, too many of our young people today are going through this horror story and their parents with them. First know that you are not alone. God knows your pain. Get down on your face. Turn to Him. You need Him to go through this. Second please, if you know a parent going through this, they need your support. Period. No matter the circumstances. As a parent their heart is breaking. Share the love of Jesus Christ. Take them to church, share the gospel. Tell them there is healing from God and restoration because Jesus Christ died on the Cross for them and they do not have to bear shame or guilt.

Our country is in crisis, with too many of our adult males incarcerated and it is no question the devil is trying to destroy our country. Nothing short of vigilant prayer, and the love of Jesus Christ is going to fight this **spiritual battle** and **it is** a **spiritual battle**! Until we wise up and fight it as a **spiritual battle against the devil who is busy trying to take our nation down,** we will not make the progress needed.

I hurt when I think of all our loved ones with an addiction who get locked up. Don't get me wrong, when you steal, deal or hurt another human being, you must pay the consequences. What my son did was wrong, but punishment does not help recovery from addiction. There has to be a better way. If you know a mother whose child with addiction is "locked up" or even a mother whose child is locked up for whatever reason, you know she has a **gaping hole** in her heart! Minister to her! Show her the love of Jesus Christ!

As I prepared to write this part of this book, I reread all the letters my son had written me while in prison. It was most difficult to read them again, but also very good. While he was locked up, he had a lot of time to reflect, and he was clean and sober. He told me in his letters that there were drugs there in prison, but obviously he chose not to use. Maybe he chose not to use for fear he would have to stay longer, or that he would be unable to protect himself. Perhaps he just didn't have the money or was not willing to do what he had to do to get the drugs. Maybe he was ready for a sober life, but for whatever his reason, he stayed clean. In one of his letters he told me that being there made him realize his freedom was vital. He also told me in his letters, that he was able to observe and learn a lot about "human choices" and reflect on his own. While he was in prison, I got to see his soul through his letters, and how much God was a part of him, and how God was working on him. Don't ever underestimate that God can show up even while our loved ones are incarcerated. It showed me how God carried him through those prison days, and how God carried me through as well.

**Carrying on….**

As for me, life carried on while my son was in prison, just as it will for other mothers. I felt it fortunate to have normalcy, doing things such as working, cleaning house, and preparing meals. But if I am honest, interacting with others or socializing was incredibly difficult due to the enormous grief I was experiencing. People who knew would ask, "Have you heard from Stephen?" I appreciated them asking, but the reminder also broke my heart. To socialize was incredibly difficult, as I was grieving.

As I have mentioned earlier, when our child has an addiction, there is a lot of grief. Grief of what we thought life would be. Sometimes without even realizing it, we dream up in our head a path we think will likely happen with our child's future, and prison is definitely not part of that scenario. As mothers we grieve for ourselves, and we hurt for them. We hurt that they have to go through this, and what it means for their future. There is a lot of pain! The only way to get through this and to get to peace and understanding on the other side, is by the peace that surpasses all understanding through God.

*Do not be anxious about anything, but in every situation, by prayer and petition, with thanksgiving, present your request to God. And the peace of God, which transcends all understanding, will guard your hearts and your minds in Christ Jesus. (Philippians 4:6-7 NIV)*

During the time that my son was in prison, I was truly blessed in that my husband helped, and because my son was the youngest of four, the older kids were out of the nest. However, the emotional, financial, and physical toll was phenomenal. The spiritual toll was grueling. As I wept, as I sobbed, and as I fought for quiet time with God (most often fighting myself, for that quiet time). something miraculous happened.

I became grateful for the concepts I had learned in Alanon about boundaries. Being unable to control the situation of him being locked up prevented me from allowing my son and his addiction to swallow me up. God gave me wisdom and understanding and reminded me that a lot of the time since Stephen's addiction had emerged, I had made him an idol in an effort to fix him. God also gave me guidance in my quiet time, to no longer do for Stephen what he could do for himself. But most importantly, God gave me healing. I spent time each and every day in prayer and praise, using my iPad to listen to Christian music. I closed my eyes and just thanked God for loving me. When the tears would flow down my checks, I would just let them flow, as I came to realize that those were tears of joy and relief of all the pain.

One last thing I came to realize about my quiet time is that in our busy lives we often can't *hear* God. In our prayer life, we often go to God and ask Him to provide for us, but we don't often take the time to "listen" to Him. He needs us to be still and quiet to *hear* Him. In that still quiet space, we are receptive to His Word, direction, and guidance. One of my favorite songs, "Speak to Me" by Kari Jobe, also helps me with that.

Listen to: "Speak to Me" by Kari Jobe

While my son was in prison, I would routinely and randomly wake up at four in the morning. At first it annoyed me, knowing I had to go to work the next morning. Then again, being a mother with a **gaping hole** of pain in my heart, I was not surprised that I could not sleep well. God laid it on my heart, that perhaps this was the only time He could speak to me in complete quiet. I decided He might have something to say. So... I got in the habit of sitting up in my bed when I awakened at four in the morning and asking God to open my ears and my heart and let me hear whatever it was, He needed me to hear. This became a very special intimate time with God for me during the hardest times. I know it helped me through.

# 14

# SURRENDER

## How to Surrender

It was around this time that I made my decision to surrender. I did not feel I could survive any more pain. My heart felt like it was torn apart. For me, surrender was a very intentional and personal commitment to work diligently on my personal relationship with God. I did this through quiet time, prayer, reading my Bible, journaling and I decided to join a women's Bible study, and prayer group. My husband and I returned to a church family. This is what worked for me. I believe if you seek an intimate relationship with your Heavenly Father, He will put you on the right path and put people on your path that will help you. When we thirst for that closeness with Him and fix our eyes, hearts, and minds on Him we are open to connecting to our Heavenly Father. The Holy Spirit will guide us to Bible studies, churches, and other Christian believers, at least that has certainly been my experience, and it can happen for you as well.

I got down on my knees and sincerely, and genuinely, asked God to take the lead in my life. I knew that I couldn't manage my life the way I had been living anymore. All of my driving the boat, basically led me in circles. I was ready to hand over the steering wheel, the reins, or the power, to God. I was tired. I was weary. I had nothing left. I surrendered. I gave up, and gave in. I asked for forgiveness for the arrogance of trying to do everything myself, including trying to save my son on my own, or my way. I had to let go of my son and give him to God completely. I felt like I was dying. I let myself be vulnerable to God, to myself, and to a few Christian friends, and my Alanon sponsor.

For a while, I didn't even feel I could fix a cup of coffee without asking Jesus to help me, but that was OK. I was starting from scratch. I put my whole life, my whole trust, my whole heart and self in God's hands and care. I recognized and really realized I could not control my son's destiny. **I could not stop my son from dying.** I was not in control, but God was, and I could trust Him with my life and my heart, no matter what happened. He would take care of me and He was and still is, my Refuge, my Protector and my Provider.

I visualized placing my son at the feet of Jesus. He was very sick using IV Heroin, and basically a ghost of himself. I knew I could not save him. I was completely powerless, and felt I was losing myself as well, into a deep pit of despair and grief. I had given up hope that he would ever be better. I felt God had forgotten me and my son until I surrendered.

Listen to the song: "Surrender" by Hillsong

**Why?**

I know it is hard, and feels somewhat counter intuitive as mothers, to "Let Go", but remember the other part. We are "Letting God" take over our loved ones with addictions. And though we may not want to admit it, God is much more capable, with many more resources, than even us mothers, right? I came to realize, on my knees, that my arrogance had kept me from letting go, while thinking that I could save my son. In my desperation, I really thought I knew best! Ha! Totally surrendering, and focusing on my relationship with God required a letting go of my son and placing him in the trustworthy arms of Jesus Christ. No more obsession, no more trying to guide my son's destiny.

From this point, it was about me focusing on mine and God's intimate relationship. Letting Go and Letting God was what I had learned about in Alanon, but really, I had no idea how to put it into action in my life. Also, at this point in my life, I was so exhausted, I didn't have the energy anymore to keep trying to micromanage my son's life!

I love my son but I had to separate my love from the attempts to rescue, control, or fix him. I had engaged in these unhealthy behaviors for years. This was not the answer and it was harming us both. I needed God's loving care and healing, and Stephen did too. Even though he had an addictive illness, a disease, I just knew I had to "Let Go and Let God" take care of him, and I needed to focus on my healing and relationship with God.

From the time our children are newborns until high school at least, we expend tons of energy trying to guide, urge, and sometimes coerce them toward a successful path. But once they start into addiction, it is a different ballgame. Letting go and giving them over to God when they are in the depths of addiction, is somewhat essential for our sanity and survival. God working on them is essential for their survival. What happens when we let go, is that we allow God to do His work with them without our interference.

Addiction by definition is a **progressive** disease meaning it gets worse as the addict or alcoholic continues to use. Therefore, we watch our loved ones get worse and worse physically, mentally, and spiritually. This is the reason that my son's addiction took me, as it does many mothers, down to my knees. It gets worse many times before it gets better, really, really worse. This is not a sensational comment, this is a fact.

## Total Surrender

We need God! We need to surrender to His power, because our human powerlessness is no match for this horrid, evil, entity that has taken over our loved one. Many addicts and alcoholics in AA or NA quote, "I am clean, 'by the Grace of God.'" They know that God swooped them up, out of the abyss and they know, that they were in the grips of the evil one. They know that without the miraculous power of God himself, they would have died. I believed I was dying of a broken, fractured, **hemorrhaging heart**, when I cried out to God to save me. I believe that God showed me I needed to get out of the way, and let him fight Stephen's battle.

Listen to "Lead me to the Cross" by Francesca Battistelli

This is a true song of beginning at your knees. Be sure to look at the lyrics.

Sometimes we hesitate to let go even though we are hurting over our **hemorrhaging gaping** hole in our heart. We may continue to hold on due to some "habit" or pattern that we have had for so long that it feels like "a part of us." For example, we have a need to control our loved one. While our loved one's addictive behavior is causing excruciating pain, we fear the pain of losing control would be worse. The need to be in control keeps us in bondage.

Again, the lack of surrender, the lack of trust in our Heavenly Father, and the lack of commitment to Him, keep freedom at bay. It can be hard for some to take that leap of faith to let go of control, and to trust God to be in control, particularly if you have been a victim of abuse in your past, and you fear that the only way not to be abused again is to stay in control. You must tell yourself that God is **Not Human**! God will never abuse you or desert you. He will not let you down. God is **TRUSTWORTHY**.

There is no peace with you in this control cycle and the **gaping hole and pain in your heart** continues to hemorrhage. If you stay in this control cycle, it becomes a self-imposed control frenzy, and a poor attempt to ward off fear and anxiety. It doesn't work. You cannot control another human being (your loved one with an addiction). There is no peace in that frenzy. The only answer is to get down on your knees, and in this case, you likely need to get down on your face before God and ask for forgiveness for a lack of faith in Him. Ask God to help you put your faith in Him allowing Him to take control one day at a time, maybe one hour at a time.

Think about it. **He** has kept you alive so far. **He** has also kept your child alive so far. **He** has provided you with food, shelter, clothing, and air to breath, not you! You have not been in control of these things! If God had wanted, He could have struck all of us down, He has that power. But He is a loving, forgiving, gracious God. He has patiently waited for each of us to put away our foolish pride and arrogance and realize that He is in control, NOT US.

So, give up your illusion of control. Stop listening to the lies in your head that you are in control. Total commitment to surrender to your Heavenly Father leads to **Total Freedom**! Acknowledge His power and control, and start asking for forgiveness for your blindness. Thank Him for ALL He has done for you, and ask Him to help you one step at a time, on this new journey of trusting Him, and learning to DEPEND ON HIM. Learn how-to live-in faith. He is patient and kind, and understands that it is a learning process. Just talk to Him every day about your fears. But stay committed to the process of surrendering to Him. Let your prayer be, "Your will Lord, not mine." He will lead you.

Listen to the song "Only Grace" by Matthew West-- God opens his Arms to you!

*Amy Shirey PA C, LPC*

# 15

# WHY DO WE NEED TO SURRENDER?...

## Getting Out of The Way

Once your loved one starts becoming defiant, and you are face to face with her addiction, and you start wondering, "Where did my child go?"- she is most likely deep into her addiction, and is not herself. She is not in control of her own actions! She is operating with a very toxic brain.

Some parents at this stage will spend hours, even months, lecturing their child to no avail. Parents will even spend months trying to figure out their loved one's actions when actually there is no logical answer. Their child is toxic and their only agenda is to get their next fix or high. The parents feel better after "the talk" and tell themselves they think it helped, or say to themselves, "I think I saw a faint light come on in her eyes", but actually, you are talking to a toxic brain and wasting time. You notice this when shortly after "the talk", you see her distance herself again and return to her previous behavior of not being interested in the family at all, and isolating in her room.

When your loved one is in periods of heavy using, you may notice money missing, spoons missing, and lies being told. Maybe you feel in your gut something is not right, or you may find substances in your loved one's room or car. Things such as pills, spoons, lighters, random belts or ropes (used for tourniquets) appear. Your loved one may get arrested, they stop obeying your rules, they come home high, or their grades are plummeting. These signs are terrifying and heart breaking.

If they are out on their own, no longer living under your roof, they never come around anymore, and they never call or return your calls unless they want money. They seem to have problems with their job or can't keep a job. They have problems with their bills and finances. They have problems with their relationships, if they have one. You often notice that things "go missing" from your home if they have access to your house.

Make sure above all things: **Do not put your head in the sand!!** And **Do not play the blame game!!** Time is of the essence. Your child's life is on the line. **This is why you surrender.** <u>You can make a difference in your life and theirs.</u> Put on your oxygen mask momma! Hopefully, their brain isn't too fried at this point. Get out of the way, let God take over. **It's time to get on your knees and ask for direction from God.** You definitely need to ask God to protect your child. The reason for surrender is to find *your* peace and to *pray* for *your* Child!

At this point, you must place boundaries on your home so that they don't steal you blind, and confront them lovingly, stating that you are aware that they have a substance problem. Be completely prepared that they will most likely deny your assertion. Tell them you will support them if they are ready to go to treatment but that you will no longer be a part of this self-destructive pathway that they are choosing. Tell your loved one, just as my old Alanon sponsor would say, "I will be part of the solution, but I will not be part of the problem." Then the most monumental thing to do, is to get down on your knees and pray for God to open your loved one's heart to a miracle.

## Spiritual Warfare

Why is it imperative to surrender? Well first, you will be going deeper into your relationship with your Heavenly Father and this is so important as you deal with what you are facing with your child. You are in the midst of **Spiritual Warfare**. Please listen to what I am about to say...We as Christians are in perilous times. While you do need to educate yourself about your child's or adult child's addiction, this is just the tip of the iceberg.

Have you not wondered on a deep spiritual level, why so many young people are dying from drug overdoses? Yes, it is true that drugs are very available, yes, some doctors are over prescribing, but on a spiritual level, a deeper level, the devil is very busy! He is busy robbing our children in as many ways as possible, and drugs and alcohol are at the top of his list! If you feel your child is not himself, he is not, he has been hijacked. This is not to scare you into a frenzy. It is to get you into spiritual warfare!

**Your surrender through prayer to your Heavenly Father is protection for your whole family!** Get on your knees before your Heavenly Father, and denounce the evil one in Jesus's name! What does this mean? Tell God you feel that Satan has attacked your family and you desperately need His help. Hopefully you are a Christian. If not, return to the front of this book and go through the steps in chapter two.

When Jesus ascended back to His Heavenly Father after His resurrection from death, God sent the Holy Spirit to live on earth in each of us believers. Jesus said in the Bible that He left within us the same authority that He had. This included telling the devil to take a hike.

*And the seventy returned again with joy, saying, Lord, even the devils are subject unto us through thy name. (Luke 10:17 KJV).*

*Behold, I give unto you power to tread on serpents and scorpions, and over all the power of the enemy: and nothing shall by any means hurt you. (Luke 10:19 KJV)*

Part of being a Christian during current times is that our religious beliefs are under attack, but we can depend on God to protect us. Jesus already won this battle by rising from His death which proved

His power over evil. This is a powerful proclamation! So, No! Satan <u>cannot</u> have your child! In Jesus name! When I felt my family was under attack, I spent many hours rebuking the devil out of my son and my family, in the name of Jesus. As a Christian you have through the power of the Holy Spirit the ability to do this also.

While in my recovery, I took a Bible study. My son was still on the streets using. The study was by Pricilla Shirer called <u>Fervent: A Woman's Battle Plan for Serious, Specific, and Strategic Prayer.</u> I highly recommend it. If your child is an IV Heroin or opioid user, nothing short of this kind of serious prayer is needed. This precious lady teaches us how to call Satan out. This addiction, that has taken many of our children to the grave, is nothing more than Satan grazing over our country, and cherry picking our young people, while rubbing his grubby little hands together, and laughing behind their mothers' backs.

Don't listen to Satan, listen to this song: "Fear is a Liar" by Zack Williams

A close walk with your God Almighty and an understanding that once you have truly accepted Jesus Christ as your Lord and Savior, and made a commitment to live for Him, means that you have the power and authority just like Christ, to denounce the evil one right out of your life, your family's life, and your child's life! For when God is with you, who can be against you? This decision to live for Christ is a life changer!

***What shall we then say to these things? If God be for us, who can be against us? (Romans 8:31 KJV)***

Don't get me wrong, my decision and deep commitment to live for Christ doesn't mean that I don't get attacked at times, but I have God on my side. Satan is not God. He cannot read my mind. He tries to use trickery, to mislead and deceive us, and he is the creator of confusion, chaos, deception, and lies. Does this sound familiar? It sounds very much like living with a loved one in the turbulence of addiction, doesn't it?

## Who Do You Want to Be Fighting for You?

I recall once, when Stephen was at home for a couple of weeks, I could feel an evil presence in the house. This was just prior to him going back into a treatment facility. Stephen and I were both contentious, argumentative, and full of anger. I was so tense. I was trying to pray the evil one out of him, and denounce the lies out of my mind that Satan was trying to get me to believe. I remember saying, "I command you Satan to get out of my bedroom, and out of my whole house, in the Name of Jesus!" My son came into my bedroom, and he was arguing with me, I think, because I would not let him use my car. I had been praying and asking, "God, why do I feel this negative energy in our home?" Suddenly, while I was listening to my son rant, and praying under my breath asking God to take this evil spirit out of my home, I envisioned at the foot of my bed and between myself and my son, a lion and a small angel. Let me just stop right here and say, that this is not a common occurrence in my life. In fact, it is the only time in my life that I have had a wide awake "vision" but, I believe and *know* to this day, that it was God showing me protection from the evilness that was taking advantage of my son in his devastating addiction, and this evilness was affecting the whole household. Even my husband said that the hostility during those two weeks in the house was palpable. Thankfully, my son was accepted into his treatment program shortly thereafter. After my son left, as my husband and I were cleaning my son's bedroom, we found evidence that he had been shooting up heroin, while awaiting his placement in treatment. How he got the drugs into the house is a mystery to me, but as a mother of an addict, I do know just how resourceful my loved one can be when he is in the grips of his addictive disease.

Later in my Christian studies, I learned that the Lion of Judah is a symbol of Jesus as the Protector. I thank God today for showing me, even in those times of extreme stress on our family, He was there for me. Once you let go of your pride and open your heart to God, and begin to study His word, you see that there are battles going on, which occur on a much bigger playing field than the simple three dimensional reality that we stay preoccupied with on this earthly plain.

What I mean by that is this; I have come to believe, in my deep spiritual walk, that there is truly a spiritual battle going on presently on this earth. The devil is very busy trying to get as many souls away from God as he can. When we are vulnerable, as our loved ones are when they are in bondage to drugs or alcohol, they are in the perfect susceptible position, for the evil one, to capitalize and step right into any lost souls and take up residence, or torment them if they are a child of God.

As a child of God, you do have protection. You have the Holy Spirit living inside of you. Working on your relationship with God helps you to know that you have guidance from the Holy Spirit. And as said earlier, you can call on the power and authority given to you by your Heavenly Father for protection of your family from evil, and leave that evil at the foot of the cross in the name of your Savior. If you have been overwhelmed due to your loved one's addiction, remember God has not forgotten you! Just get down on your knees and surrender to Him.

The devil gladly uses any vulnerability to pull us from Christ, not just drugs and alcohol. He will hold you hostage if you fall into sins of idolatry to people, materialism, pride over worldly success, or greed, the list goes on. These are easy distractions to turn to for those of us who are hurting as a result of our loved ones having addictions. The devil will capitalize on these susceptible sins. But remember Christ has already won the battle against evil when He rose from the dead. If you are a Christian and have the Holy Spirit living within, Satan has **no power over you**.

There are times I felt that the devil was responsible for putting on me an "ungodly spirit" of oppression or hopelessness. This can be very agonizing and frustrating as a Christian. It feels very defeating and like nothing is going in a positive way. The evil one loves to "mess with us" that way. These ungodly spirits can be so tormenting that they even make it hard to pray, and can take our focus off of God. That is the very moment that we must get down on our knees, ask for forgiveness for losing focus, ask for cleansing, and reconnect with our Heavenly Father's love and His word. We must claim God's message that Christ who rose from the grave won over evil. Read your Scripture at this point to remind you of God's love and promises and His Almighty power.

*Be sober, be vigilant; because your adversary the devil, as a roaring lion, walketh about, seeking whom he may devour: (1Peter 5:8 KJV).*

*Since the children have flesh and blood, he too shared in their humanity so that by his death he might break the power of him who holds the power of death--that is, the devil-- (Hebrews 2:14 NIV)*

*Teach me to do your will, for you are my God; may your good Spirit lead me on level ground. For your name's sake, Lord, preserve my life; in your righteousness, bring me out of trouble. In your unfailing love, silence my enemies; destroy all my foes, for I am your servant. (Psalm 143:10-12 NIV)*

The bottom line is this: If you stay focused on your relationship and daily walk with God, as you are dealing with your life with your loved one having an addiction, you are definitely in a position of protection. That is **why** you need to surrender. You are not vulnerable to Satan, because God is stronger and more powerful than the evil one. As a Christian you have God to carry you through this horrific ordeal and any other struggle. He will provide for you, protect you, and heal you. You have Him to turn to and pray to for protection and healing of your child. We can pray for our children and for our peace, like the victorious Saints of God that we have been empowered to be. When we walk this walk, we can expect to be successful in this serious battle!

*How God anointed Jesus of Nazareth with the Holy Spirit and power, and how He went around doing good and healing all who were under the power of the devil, because God was with him. (Acts 10:38 NIV)*

## Do Not Be Afraid

In Ms. Shirer's book she recommends we must bow down, repent our sins, and have the courage to trust and walk in His way through prayer and reading His Word. When we do this, we walk in freedom and not in fear! As a mother with that **gaping hole** in my heart, I was often held back due to fear.

When we bow down and repent that we have fear, and truly have faith that God has us in His arms, whatever His plan may be, we will be freed. The Holy Spirit in us will give us the power to change our thoughts (those lies) and we will truly come to believe and have faith in God's plan instead of fearing "what might happen."

Through our belief in Christ we must resist the devil's attempt to get us to believe lies about ourselves. For me, these lies included things like, my child's addiction was my fault, or I should be able to stop my child from using, the list goes on and on. I have also learned that the devil works overtime trying to get us to believe the lies about our loved ones with addictions. Examples of this would be, "He's never going to change," or "He'll never get better." I was even guilty of saying things like, "He's sorry, or lazy," and would fall into thinking, "He doesn't love me anymore," or "He doesn't love his family anymore."

This is the reason we must stay focused on Christ, and strive to have a pure mind and heart. But as a new Christian, and while in the midst of the storm of living with a loved one with an addiction, it can be very difficult to fight those lies in your mind. This is especially true if we have an argumentative, manipulative addict in the home. We are so vulnerable. Quite frankly, this is when a loving accepting group of Christian prayer warriors can remind you that those lies are from the devil and that God is a lot stronger than the devil! We need the help and support of Alanon sponsorship and education, but most importantly we need our Lord and Savior Jesus Christ holding us up and a strong Christian church family.

*Because greater is he that is you than he that is in the world.*
*(1 John 4:4 KJV)*

In my prayer life, each and every time these lies came into my mind, I began breaking agreement with the devil, and I would tell him I would no longer agree to his lies. I reminded myself that I was a child of God, and the evil one had NO authority over me or my son who was also a Christian and a child of God. In my quiet time with God, I praised Him, and I rejoiced in the fact that I believed in **victory** not defeat! I am thankful that Alanon broke down healthy common-sense coping skills for me, but my spiritual warrior prayer life and my faith in my Heavenly Father was what helped me survive what was overwhelming at first.

I now see, years later and after much Bible study, the importance of casting out those lies of the enemy from one's mind. When you cast out the lies of the enemy from your mind about your loved one, your faith strengthens, and that along with the skills of self-care, creates more faith and hope.

Prayer with faith and the assurance that Jesus has already won the victory over evil is coming from a very different place than prayer from fear. If you are praying from fear, I recommend you find yourself some strong Christian women, prayer warriors, who you can connect with and learn about the power of the Holy Spirit. He will answer prayers sent up for your loved ones. The Lord says in His Word,

*For where two or three are gathered together in my name, there am I in the midst of them. (Matthew 18:20 KJV)*

*For God has not given us the spirit of fear; but of power, and of love, and of a sound mind. (2 Timothy 1:7 KJV)*

In the book of Hebrews, we are also told to never give up hope. And a close walk with God will show that is definitely possible. Alanon encourages to "Let Go and Let God" and to "Take it One Day at a Time." Alanon also encourages at the beginning to have a regular conscience contact with God which can lead you to your Savior's arms.

I recall listening to the Christian song "Oceans" by Hillsong which talks about God taking me to places in my faith that I would never go. Well, because of my son's addiction, I believe God has done that. I did not believe that I could ever "Let Go and Let God." I did not believe I could ever be at peace with God either taking my son to heaven, or getting him sober without my involvement. For me, that would be soaring to a place I hadn't been before. For me, it did take much time with God, many conversations in prayer with Him, and many tears, sobs, and on my knees time. But God has patience. God led me to those deep waters step by step.

Listen to "Oceans" by Hillsong

# COMMITMENT

**Full Time Versus Part Time**

Coming to Christ is meant to be a full-time commitment. I think of the book of Genesis. You know the guy Noah, who built the ark? Whoa, what a commitment. It took him a long time, and you know he was ridiculed. My point is, you cannot connect with God part time, or every now and then, or just when your child has to go to court, and expect to get the kind of results that will bring you peace. This relationship with God has to be a longing, a desire, a need in your life. You have to want it.

You may seem a bit different to others, as you walk this walk, you can feel you are different inside, because as God begins working on you, you do change. Your heart becomes softer and kinder and you make different choices. You see things differently. You begin to see things the way God sees things. This comes with the territory. But the **gaping hole** in your heart well, it begins to heal, and that peace that surpasses all understanding, well, just wait for it. And the pain, over time, will actually begin to hurt less. The apostle Paul gave up everything to follow Christ. (Philippians 3:8) If you could have peace in your situation with your loved one's addiction, would you follow Paul's lead?

Listen to "The Motions" by Matthew West

This is how I felt. I had to jump in head first, and develop a direct connection of prayer to God to survive.

**Old Behavior Begone Beware!**

Don't let those old behavior patterns, due to anger or fear, keep you from making the commitment that will heal that **gaping hole in**

**your heart** that continues to hemorrhage. The only answer is to get down on your knees before the Holy One. All else keeps you in bondage. Don't let your lack of faith that God has nothing better for you, keep you stuck. God loves His children and wants more than anything for you to live a life of peace and prosperity (Jeremiah 20:11-13). Even a little faith can grow. I prayed for God to grow my faith and put the work into prayer and studying His Word and my prayer was answered. It is amazing how good God is when we choose to take that leap of faith and listen to Him and follow His guidance.

*For I know the plans I have for you, declares the Lord, 'plans to prosper you and not to harm you, plans to give you hope and a future. (Jeremiah 29:11 NIV)*

**Repentance**

There is always room for repentance.

*Repent, then, and turn to God, so that your sins may be wiped out, that times of refreshing may come from the Lord, (Acts 3:19 NIV)*

Just before I made my **total** commitment, I took a "fearless inventory" of myself (this is the fourth step in Alanon) with my sweet elderly sponsor. I humbly looked back at my life as a "luke warm" follower of Christ. I was so ashamed of some of the things I had done in my twenties and even thirties. I just started balling. I was acutely aware of the fact that Jesus had done nothing wrong in His life. He was totally innocent, yet stepped up to the plate, took a beating, was ridiculed, spit on, nailed to a wooden cross, a criminal's death really, all for me. I should have been in that place. He took that, for me. He did that for you too. No questions asked. No regrets. God's plan, unbelievable! It still rocks me when I think about it, to this day. If God loved us enough to give His son, we can surely rest assured that our future is hopeful and bright. All He wants is for us to live for Him. He is the creator of the Universe and He seeks us! Salvation is an unbelievable gift to be embraced and celebrated every day! We can rejoice that we are no longer heading to hell, but are living as inheritors of the Holy Kingdom!

Listen to the song, "Just be Held" by Casting Crowns

## When Trouble Comes

So, in your committed walk with Christ, when troubles come, as it often does when your loved one has an addiction, you have a solid foundation, you know you can turn to your Heavenly Father for guidance, comfort, healing, and protection. You must take the steps to come to Him, in order for Him to give you rest.

*Come to me, all you who are weary and burdened, and I will give you rest. (Matthew 11:28 NIV)*

*Amy Shirey PA C, LPC*

# 17

# THE BENEFITS OF SURRENDERING

I had come to believe that I absolutely could not survive the gaping hole in my heart anymore. I could not do it without God's help. I had to stop doing things my way. God changed my beliefs, helping me to see that He loved me enough to help me. He will do this for you.

These benefits I received; you may receive also. You can begin to have hope again for the first time in years. You can come to realize that God really loves you, and He will provide you with blessings, so it is really ok to hope for a positive future. This may sound trivial, but for years sometimes we are in bondage of "unbelief" actually believing things will never get better. Are you ready to **REALLY** believe that your life can get better, your child **CAN** get better, the dark cloud over you can move, and you and you family can be covered, protected by the blood of Jesus? And that just as it says in Jeremiah God has plans to prosper you?

**God's Love**

Also, based on the realization of His love, you will come to realize, really realize, just how much He loves you based on His giving **His only Son** to forgive you of your sins. Are you ready to spend some time concentrating on the fact that God gave His only Son up to die a criminal, painful, tortuous death so that your sins could be forgiven? God loves you so much and by virtue of you putting your trust and faith in Him, and asking Christ in to your life, you are washed white as snow of your sins and are receiving God's love and protection.

## God's Healing

He will show you that if you put your faith in Him, not yourself, as painful as it is to accept that you have no power over your loved one's addiction, He will show you that you can trust Him. You can pour out in prayer and tears, all your pain from your loved one's addiction, as well as every other betrayal that you have ever experienced in your life, and He will heal you.

You can lay all the pain of your heart at the foot of the cross and get really raw with God about all the times people have left you, rejected you, or hurt you in any way. Just allow your loving precious Heavenly Father to swoop you up in His arms to heal you. It is there for the taking. Just bravely trust and step into the sacred space of prayer with your Heavenly Father and ask for healing. He will teach you how to begin to detect lies being told to you, that are not from Him, and then show you the lies that you have been telling yourself, about yourself.

## Learning How to Fight

You can learn when you have been deceived by the evil one and how to stand up to the evil one by the power that you have inherited as a Child of God and the Holy Spirit who lives in you. You will begin to feel empowered by the power of the Holy Spirit to denounce that evil one out of your family's life and tell it to go to the foot of the cross in the name of Jesus. It has no power over you as a Child of God! Your Heavenly Father, through the Holy Spirit, will also, over time, reveal to you the concept of spiritual warfare, and how to discern the evil one busily working in our world today, and how to kick that evil one to the curb.

Some years ago, I resisted the concept of the "evil one" or the devil. I realized that I had always strongly believed in the Holy Spirit, even growing up as a Christian and as a child, but for some reason I felt ashamed or embarrassed to acknowledge that there could be an evil spirit. I wouldn't even say "the devil" aloud for fear of being ridiculed. You know, I would be considered "wacky". People think you are crazy if you believe in the devil or angels. God opened my heart and my mind to the spiritual realm, and basically helped me to not be so narrow minded. He convicted me in my prayer time, and led me to His Holy Word. He showed me the numerous scriptures and references to the Holy Spirit's presence, angels, and yes, the devil. He even reminded me of Jesus's interactions with the devil. He was clearly preparing me for my life ahead in so many ways and so many areas.

## Your Identity

Another unexpected, but inevitable benefit of surrendering and deepening your relationship with God is that you begin to explore and better understand your identity in Christ. This is your **real** identity, not an identity based on worldly impressions like the way you look on the outside, or your family's status or wealth. Your true identity is based on the fact that as a believer, you are a Child of God.

Once you accept that you are powerless over your loved one's addiction, and you surrender and "Let Go and Let God," you begin to realize that maybe there is more to you than just a rescuer of your child from this horrendous addiction. Maybe your loved one and God are in charge of the rescue. Maybe, there is more that defines you and your future. But once you begin to try to identify yourself outside the parameters of a caretaker or rescuer, many mothers don't really know who they are, know what to do with themselves, or where to start to figure this out.

Of course, it can be very tempting at this juncture to just substitute another idol or project into your life. It is such a comfortable, familiar behavioral pattern to pick up a project or idol, right? However, most mothers are very tired and weary and are in dire need of rest. This can actually be an advantage in that it might prevent them from getting sucked back into another project, and this rest time is the perfect opportunity to seek God and heal. At this crossroad, hopefully, instead of taking on another project during this period of fatigue and exhaustion, we mothers can learn to sit still and quiet and work on our close relationship with God.

When you begin to deeply think about your identity in your Savior you might be drawing a blank, I certainly did at first, but bear with me. And Let's look at some scripture.

> *You did not choose me, but I chose you and appointed you so that you might go and bear fruit—fruit that will last--and so that whatever you ask in my name the Father will give you. (John 15:16 NIV)*

> *But you are a chosen people, a royal priesthood, a holy nation, God's special possession, that you may declare the praises of him who called you out of darkness into his wonderful light. (1 Peter 2:9 NIV)*

> *If God is for us, who can be against us? (Romans 8:31b NIV)*

> *For he chose us in him before the creation of the world to be holy and blameless in his sight. In love he predestined us for adoption to sonship through Jesus Christ, in accordance with his pleasure and will-to the praise of his glorious grace, which he has freely given us in the One he loves. (Ephesians 1: 4-6 NIV)*

You see it is no mistake that you are at this point in your life, looking and seeking answers. It is no surprise God is seeking you. So, as you wonder how you will survive the pain and how you will fill the void in your heart and soul, once you "Let Go and Let God" take care of your loved one, you will begin to recognize God is seeking YOU. He wants to heal **you** and to fill **you**, and to remind **you** who you really are, "A Child of God."

- You are important to God.

- What is important to you, is important to God.

- You are valuable to God (all of God's children are).

- You matter to God.

- You are chosen by God.

- You are forgiven by God.

- You are loved by God.

- You are an heir to the Holy Kingdom.

- You are God's child,

- His daughter or His son.

- You are freed from your sins by the blood of Jesus.

- He knows your name!

- You are wanted by your Father.

- You are held in treasure by God.

- You are adored by God your Father.

- You are His forever.

Now read this list repeatedly. Digest it, claim it, pray over it, so that it will become not just thoughts, but beliefs. You must come to accept the assurance of God's love for you, and your identity as a child of God and an heir to the Holy Kingdom.

Listen to the song: "He Knows My Name" by Francesca Battistelli.

God will show you your true identity as a Child of God. Also, in the Word, is scripture that verifies our identity as heirs to God's Kingdom as His children.

***Listen, my dear brothers and sister: Has not God chosen those who are poor in the eyes of the world to be rich in faith and to inherit the kingdom he promised those who love him? (James 2:5 NIV)***

## His Protection

We have talked a lot about the power of the Holy Spirit who lives within us, once we become believers of Christ. With this power of the Holy Spirit we have the power to denounce the devil out of our lives, and as I have said before, we can then send him to the curb! But I want to discuss God's direct protection, His protection that is going on day and night, twenty-four hours a day, seven days a week. God never sleeps. He is never surprised by the enemy. He sees the enemy coming long before we do. He sends His angels to protect us.

Listen to the song, "Defender" by Rita Springer

***I lift up my eyes to the mountains--where does my help come from? My help comes from the Lord, the Maker of heaven and earth. He will not let your foot slip--he who watches over you will not slumber; (Psalm 121:1-3 NIV)***

As a believer of Jesus Christ, we can rest assured that we are promised a life covered under the protection of God and His angels. We are promised that nothing can separate us from His love, no matter what we face. He is our provider and protector. He uses His angels to watch over and protect us. Angels are cited all throughout the Bible for their amazing ability to protect those in harm's way. So, as a child of God, this is our gift, and as mothers of children with addiction, we can certainly pray that God sends His angels of protection over our children. Based on the many dangerous situations my son was in, I am certain God and His angels protected him.

*For he will command his angels concerning you to guard you in all your ways; (Psalm 91:11 NIV)*

*The angel of the Lord encamps around those who fear him, and he delivers them. (Psalm 34:7 NIV)*

*The Lord will rescue me from every evil attack and will bring me safely to his heavenly kingdom. To him be glory for ever and ever. Amen. (2 Timothy 4:18 NIV)*

You can commit yourself fervently to your walk with God in intimacy, which will definitely make you hungry for a deeper study of His Word. And as you do that, you will feel His protection from Satan. As a Christian, we can all rest assured in faith that we are covered by the blood of Jesus who has already won the battle against Satan.

God showed me that He absolutely would not **ever** leave me, and would protect me, and provide for me, from the beginning of this vulnerable ordeal, all the way through the healing process. Then, as I grew in my relationship, growing closer to my Lord, I got stronger, and wanted more understanding and more time with God. The amazing thing is that I always continuously felt His protection. On this journey you will get stronger and stronger in your walk with Christ and gain more and more benefits and blessings because that is what happens when you walk in closeness to God.

God gave me heart felt insight into the horrific sacrifices that His Son Jesus made for me. He continues to help me understand the importance of asking daily for MORE faith, and a closer walk day by day. But God also showed me in a very loving way, some areas of my life that I needed to improve or clean up. As I said earlier, your life will change and you will feel different in your heart. Sometimes, it is a result of a revelation from your Heavenly Father. I continually thank God for the gifts of wisdom, knowledge, and discernment that

He has given me, and pray that He will continue to strengthen these gifts so that I may use them to glorify Him.

# 18

# A CHANGE IN ME, A CHANGE IN YOU

## Dependency on God

After you fall to the floor in total despair, and plead to God for help in hopelessness, helplessness, and lack of control over your love one's condition (which correlates with the 1st step in Alanon, "our powerlessness"), the Holy Spirit **will** lead you. I began to see that I had been making an idol of my son of sorts, by putting all my attention and conscious intentions on his life, while basically ignoring my close personal relationship to God. I had been ignoring my need to recognize my dependency on my Heavenly Father. While that was not an easy revelation to accept, and it was a stomach punch deep inside, I could feel the truth behind it. I knew I could do nothing without God. How long I had tried to depend on myself! How hard headed can one be? And while I knew there was truth within, I had no idea how to change my self-reliance, or what my life would look like or be like if I changed it. But praise God, God was about to show me.

## No More Idols

In my quiet time with God, He reminded me in a very loving way of His Commandment: Thou shall place no other God's before Me (Exodus 20:3 NIV). I realized that for years, my primary focus had been on my son's life, even well into his adulthood. I had been so wrapped up in trying to fix him, rescue him, control him, convince him of doing what *I thought* he needed to do, that I had made him my project, my life's goal, so to speak. Many mothers do this, but we can especially fall into this behavior pattern when our child is in the grips of her addiction. We feel fearful, then hopeless, and make our child an idol. This is the behavioral pattern that we adopt due to that fear, and due to the realization of loss of control. Even if our child or adult child gets clean and sober for a while, we might make it our goal to *keep* her on track. This is actually the same thing; we are still making her our idol. We then become obsessed with her recovery program and our efforts turn to trying to "keep her sober." We still totally lose our focus of any and everything else, but most importantly we lose our focus from our **Heavenly Father**.

When our children are little, and growing into toddlers, then elementary school, then middle school, then high school, and we are directing their life activities and friends, we feel in control, but truthfully, we are NOT. Just ask a mother whose child gets cancer. She will tell you; it is God who is in control. This feeling of control, that we think we have, is an illusion. That illusion gives us a false sense of pride and arrogance, depending on ourselves, instead of God. I am reminded of the story of Abraham in the Bible when he took his son Isaac, at God's direction, and laid him on an altar and was about to sacrifice him to God. He was actually instructed by God to take his son's life, to give, as a sacrifice to God, then God stopped him. Wow! Now that's devotion and obedience to God!

Maybe we moms do need to pause and reflect, looking at our commitment to God versus our commitment to our children. I had gotten so wrapped up in saving my son myself, but what about my relationship to God? What was I doing for God? When did I stop and ask God, "What can I do for you today God?" or "How can I serve you?"

Being totally wrapped up in our obsession with our loved one's chaotic life of addiction will absolutely consume us to exhaustion. Now don't get me wrong, I believe God has compassion for us while we are grieving, and He is so very sad about the self-destructive path our children are pursuing. I know that because that is His nature, and He healed my broken heart and soul, and helped me get back up. I see countless other mothers in the same condition. They are hurting and grieving over their children with the disease of addiction, and desperately need help from God and love from all of us, but what they need most is healing from our loving Heavenly Father. Until we receive that ultimate healing, until we turn our eyes and heart to God for help, we remain tormented. He will show us the way. He will show us how to put our loved one's disease in His perspective, and how to see it from His eyes. This is where we receive our peace.

## Clarity of Your Purpose

For years, I had not really thought about God's purpose for my life. I was engulfed with the purpose of saving my son. After a good amount of healing time, God began to open my eyes and heart to hear that He had other plans for me. These were plans that I previously had completely been unable to hear and had blocked out, as I had tirelessly grinded on in my march to "save" my son from his addiction. Retrospectively, I see the arrogance and my lack of obedience and how I was leaving God out of the equation. I was also most likely, interfering with God and my son's walk.

Listen to the song; "Come as You Are" by Crowder

## No More Unbelief

I also learned a very valuable lesson on this journey about "unbelief." Watching my son's self-destructive path, my discouragement was building. As I previously eluded to, I often verbalized to myself and even out loud things such as, "He is never going to change," or "He is going to die." Sometimes, I actually didn't realize I was falling into unbelief and often we do this unconsciously. As mentioned earlier, the devil often whispers these phrases in our mind, but we don't have to be in agreement with him. That is partnering with unbelief and partnering with the evil one. Do not do it!

I would hear myself say or I even would tell myself," I have lost my son." Basically, I was giving up. That attitude is an attitude of **unbelief** and is a sin. God revealed that I was committing a sin on my part. Did you hear me? Even when we are facing what feels and looks absolutely terrifying, we must have faith in God that He can work a miracle out of a horrid situation if we place our faith in Him. Just look at Jesus's situation as the example.

*Fixing our eyes on Jesus, the pioneer and perfecter of faith. For the joy set before him he endured the cross, scorning its shame, and sat down at the right hand of the throne of God. Consider him who endured such opposition from sinners, so that you will not grow weary and lose heart. In your struggle against sin, you have not yet resisted to the point of shedding your blood. (Hebrews 12:2-4 NIV)*

Jesus, even being aware that He faced a criminal's death by crucifixion, went forward in faith because He loved us and believed it was God's will, and He knew His place would be at the right side of His Father in the end. He **believed** in what was **beyond the cross**. He didn't let himself get marred down in **unbelief** or the nitty, pity thoughts about what was going on, and boy was there a lot going on with His situation (being beaten, taunted, and nailed to the cross). Can you imagine the faith that took? We must make Jesus our example, instead of getting marred down into the situation of our loved one's addiction. Do not buy into the **unbelief** that Satan loves for us to hang on to. Hold fast to **belief** in our Heavenly Father who promises His children that He will **never** leave them (John 14:18) and has plans to prosper them (Jeremiah 29:11).

So, you see, your Savior went through a horrendous pre-death and death experience holding on to faith in His father. You must make this an example and have faith in God that He can carry you through the pain of your loved one's addiction. You must believe as Christ believed, in God's plan not your plan. Pray for your child, and focus on what God has for you in your life and the future plans God has for your child's life. Ask God to help you endure the race without unbelief by staying close to your Heavenly Father. Look forward to the reward of closeness to Him. You never know how He will work in your life or the life of your loved one. Jesus held on to His belief all the way to the end of the mission. We must have faith like Christ that God will come through for us. Until the end means as long as it takes! Keep praying and never give up! Talk to your child about the love of Christ and pray for laborers to come into your child's life to minister to her.

> *I will not leave you as orphans; I will come to you. (John 14:18 NIV)*

> *For I know the plans I have for you, declares the Lord, plans to prosper you and not to harm you, plans to give you hope and a future. (Jeremiah 29:11 NIV)*

God **wants** us to succeed! Just keep working on your relationship with God. Remember, God seeks us out! Both you and your child. No matter how bad our circumstances, we need to hold on to our faith, by remembering God loves us and cares for us. Have faith that God has good plans for us and wants to prosper us. So, if we are buying into these negative beliefs that are often planted in our minds by Satan himself, and if we are partnering with the evil one and practicing the sin of unbelief, we must hit our knees and ask for forgiveness, then tell Satan he has no power over us as a child of God!

In Hebrews chapter 3 verse 15 there is also a warning about us not hardening our hearts. If we go too long with unbelief in our hearts, continually saying those negative things about our loved ones, in that negativity, our hearts will be hardened and we will be, "falling away from the living God." Thus, there is no light in our heart and it is full of scars and pain. This is a true sign that the restoration and healing of Jesus is needed. It is not uncommon to get to this point after years of unrelenting pain from watching our child go through the difficult road of addiction. That pain is often tied to lies and betrayal, but there is hope. God can heal you from these scars and renew your hardened heart with a heart of flesh.

*I will give you a new heart and put a new spirit in you; I will remove from you your heart of stone and give you a heart of flesh. (Ezekiel 36:26 NIV)*

Have you ever experienced being around someone like that? They are so full of negativity that it is difficult to be around them. This can definitely be the case of parents of loved ones with addiction that are full of negativity from a hardened heart of unbelief. They have no hope and no belief that God will help them or their child. This is an excellent opportunity to minister to your brother or sister who has a gaping hemorrhaging hole in their heart. The Bible encourages us to encourage each other and this is certainly needed as we struggle with our children with addictions. God is bigger than any obstacle including a hardened heart. If you have a hardened heart from years of pain, ask God to give you a heart of flesh, and heal you. Begin to turn your pain over to Him. If you know someone who is struggling with this issue due to their child's addiction or due to any reason, pray for them and ask that God will prick their heart and give them a heart of flesh. Never stop believing that God has great things in store for you as a believer!

*See to it, brothers and sisters, that none of you has a sinful, unbelieving heart that turns away from the living God. But encourage one another daily, as long as it is called today, so that none of you may be hardened by sin's deceitfulness. We have come to share in Christ, if indeed we hold our original conviction firmly to the very end. As has just been said:*

*Today, if you hear his voice, do not harden your hearts as you did in the rebellion. (Hebrews 3:12-15 NIV)*

In the Bible there is a woman Sarah, wife of Abraham, who wanted a baby. God granted her a baby at age ninety. Needless to say, she was surprised. But what if she had given up! Never say never! God can do anything!! Have faith until the end!

The Holy Spirit really convicted me about my **unbelief.** I realized that I had become hopeless about my son due to the sin of unbelief. If I was truly a believer, where was my faith in God? The Bible was telling me to have faith **until the end.** The Bible was reminding me that even Jesus, who came to this earth and had to face a horrible death, and obviously had moments of "feelings" about it, referenced by His prayer just prior to His capture (John 12:27-28), maintained His faith. Facing what He had to face needed to be my example. I hit my knees and asked for forgiveness and began praying for God to help my son, and give me more faith.

*Now my soul is troubled, and what shall I say? Father, save me from this hour? No, it was for this very reason I came to this hour. Father, glorify your name! (John 12:27-28 NIV)*

*And without faith it is impossible to please God, because anyone who comes to him must believe that he exists and that he rewards those who earnestly seek him. (Hebrews 11:6 NIV)*

Listen to song: "Remember" by Lauren Daigle

*Amy Shirey PA C, LPC*

# 19

# MY PEACE

## The Garden

I love the song "The Garden," by Kari Jobe, singer and songwriter. It is one of the many Christian music songs that I listen to that helps me find my peace. In "The Garden," Kari sings first about being in despair at her lowest point. As mothers with children with addictions we can all relate. Then she sings "and then I saw the garden." She sings about the greenery and how God planned ahead for her moment of despair by planting the Garden for her benefit.

I have always loved nature to include the different shades of greens of the trees against the blues of the sky, and I have often thanked God for the beauty of a sunset, a full moon, and the foliage of fall. All of those gifts of nature, He planned so far ahead during creation for us! She goes on to sing "Look at the ivy growing through the wall, because You will stop at nothing to heal my broken soul." I previously worked at a building that had a brick courtyard. There was ivy in that courtyard that truly grew sporadically through that brick wall. It caught my attention and amazed me as to how in the world, that live plant could find its way through that thick brick wall into that courtyard. Kari celebrated it best in her song! That ivy is a beautiful metaphor for God's love. "He will stop at nothing to heal our broken soul!"

## The Word

Also, in search of my peace, I often read my Bible… that sacred book that has been handed down for centuries. Do you own anything that has been handed down? How many generations? Two? Three? Think of the miracle of how far and how many generations the Bible has been passed down. The miraculous Word of God has survived. Praise God! Do you know that the Word of God will come right off the page specifically with a message for you when you open and read it? It is alive today. God will speak to you specifically through His Word. Just ask Him to speak to you through His Word. All you have to do is open it. How exciting is that?

> *For the word of God is alive and active. Sharper than any doubled-edged sword, it penetrates even to dividing soul and spirit, joints and marrow; (Hebrews 4:12a NIV)*

**Slow Down and Weep**

As I have previously alluded to, my healing required a lot of Christian praise music, prayer and being in nature. During my quiet time with God sometimes I cried out to God, sometimes I screamed, sometimes I sobbed, sometimes I pleaded for God to take my pain, but He always listened and slowly I began to feel better, and eventually I felt peace. It does take time and it takes quiet time with the Lord, asking for His healing love. It's all about that **gaping hole** in your heart.

Obviously, working on my relationship with God was very connected to how devoted I was to my quiet time. As a result of this routine, some pretty magnificent things began to happen. I felt a conviction to slow down, and really take care of myself, something that I had been neglecting for several years. I chose each morning, to carve out at least thirty minutes to one hour before work, to be with God. Sometimes just to pray, sometimes to listen to praise music, sometimes to write a letter to God, and sometimes to read my Bible. It was amazing how this strengthened my faith, and how this healed me. The shock slowly wore off, and the tears began to flow. To weep initially felt uncomfortable but with time I began to realize to weep was a part of the healing process. This precious time felt so nurturing that I found myself wanting more of it in my day. I ended up seeking it out at bedtime as well.

*Record my misery; list my tears on your scroll- are they not in your record? Then my enemies will turn back when I call for help. By this I will know that God is for me. (Psalm 56:8-9 NIV)*

## Seek It and It's Inevitable

My time with my Heavenly Father provided spiritual healing and a step of growth in the deepest and most profound way. It has taken me deeper and closer to God than I could ever imagine. To some it may sound strange, or even impossible, but it is inevitable. If you pray and tell God that you desire to seek a close relationship to Him, you are actually praying for an intimacy with your Heavenly Father. Amazing things will happen. Nothing pleases Him more than when God sees His children reaching out to Him.

Of course, I still prayed diligently for my son, as he continued on his tortuous path of addiction. I prayed that God would protect him, and speak to his heart, but I asked for guidance for my life from the Holy Spirit, and read God's Word. My primary focus became my relationship with my Heavenly Father and as a result, inwardly, I felt a softening, a sense of protection, and slowly a peace came over me. This was only the beginning.

*Amy Shirey PA C, LPC*

# 20

# LEARNING TO TRUST

## Fear as An Obstacle

Before I started this intimate journey, I suppose you could say I, like many, definitely had trust issues. I trusted that God could perform miracles. I definitely believed that, I just didn't think He would do that for me. Sometimes, I just felt that God had maybe just "lost my file." Have you ever felt like that before? Like maybe God just has so much to do, He doesn't have time to worry with you? I even think I felt this way long ago, as a child. Miracles were for everyone else, not for me. On my journey, I had to dig very deep into God's love for me before I could trust Him. I began to ask myself, "Why does God love me? Why would He?"

## Am I Worthy?

In the Bible it says He created us out of love. (1 John 3:1) Have you ever made anything you really loved? Anything? A craft? A cake? A wooden box? Written a song? Or put together a project, like a painting maybe? Have you ever done so just because you wanted to and loved it? Can you imagine that God did that when He created us? He created us and loves us as His creation, period. His love for us is not based on what we do, or what we produce, or what we say, or even what we look like. He loves us at ground zero, just because we are His creation. Then He gives us free will to chose to believe in Him and chose to want to please Him or not! Which by the way, if we choose Him, makes Him very happy. But that's our choice.

*See what great love the Father has lavished on us, that we should be called children of God! And that is what we are!*

***The reason the world does not know us is that it did not know him. (1 John 3:1 NIV)***

Just stop and think for a moment about the amazing gift that you were created out of God's love for you. He then gave you dominion over this incredibly beautiful world. It really makes you realize that we have a loving God and good Father. I mentioned earlier just how much I love the ocean and fall foliage that God gave us, but God is so good He thought of everything! He also gave us one another, well knowing, we would want to belong to one another. And then, there's the **BIG ONE**! He gave us **HIS SON**! Who would do that?

Who would do that? Who would sacrifice their son? Could you do that? I honestly can't imagine doing that. By giving His Son, we are offered a choice to believe in God's only Son, who died on a cross, after terrible punishment, for our sins. Ok, are you getting the picture of just how much you are loved? How much God has given and done for you?! Just to show His love!

## Step by Step

So…Our part is to accept Jesus Christ as our Savior in our heart, believe in Him, and trust…That's a pretty small part in comparison, Right? Yes? No? Maybe? The decision may be easy, but the follow through is everything!

Putting your trust every day, every minute, sometimes minute by minute in God, is where the action comes in, and if you have had trouble trusting humans as I have, you get to realize this is a whole different situation, because for **once** in your life **you will not be let down!**

This time, you are trusting GOD. He is trustworthy. He will not let you down. He will not forsake you. He is not human. He is infallible. He loves you, and wants the best for you, even when you don't know what the best is for yourself, God knows!

I started with a little trust that God would help my son, and I prayed for God to grow my trust and faith. As I worked each and every day to follow His guidance, He helped me. Since we are human, we must stay focused on our Lord and Savior, and use the Word (Bible) to help build our faith.

Listen to the song: "Cry Out to Jesus" by Third Day

When I felt God tell me to write this book about a mother's **gaping hole** in her heart as she watches her child in the grips of addiction, I would begin at times, to feel a bit "insecure" and lack trust in my abilities. I would say to God, "God, you know that I am a math and science gal, not an English and literature person!" And I would hear, "With God all things are possible!" (Matt. 19:26). In other words, trust Me, Amy. I would also hear, "Then the Lord reached out his hand and touched my mouth and said to me, "I have put my words in your mouth" (Jeremiah 1: 9). I knew God was telling me that He would give me the words to write and that I was just supposed to be the vessel. I then would ask God, "So, God, why does my human mind have to be so scared?" and I'd pray, "Lead me Holy Spirit," (Psalm143:10). Sometimes we have to pray for God to give us greater faith especially when charged with a job that we don't necessarily feel we are equipped to handle. But that is exactly when God takes the wheel and shows us just how much we can trust Him. Because we cannot do it without Him, He shows us He is there for us and He will not let us down.

*Teach me to do your will, for you are my God; may your good Spirit lead me on level ground. (Psalm 143:10 NIV)*

*Amy Shirey PA C, LPC*

# 21

# A MOTHER'S WARNING

## A Dry Run

One day while working in my clinic, I received a call on my cell phone. I heard a muffled voice. In my panicked mind, I was convinced that it was my son, and he was trying to tell me that he had taken an overdose. You have to realize, I was well aware that in our country, our children and our adult children were dying in very high numbers of heroin and opioid overdoses. Later, I found out it was a cousin whose phone was in her pocket and she had "butt dialed" me. But my initial reaction is a great example of how hyper alert we become when we are living with an addict, and we begin to fall into "waiting for the next bad thing to happen." My panic was also likely due to the spiral of self-destruction I could see going on right in front of my face. I completely fell apart. I couldn't even use my cell phone to call 911. My nurse, Debbye, who I worked with, basically had to pick me up off the floor of the parking garage. When I finally found out it was not my son's demise, I went home and spent four hours in prayer. What God told me was, "Amy, if Stephen does overdose, you probably will not be with him, but guess what? I will be, so hit your knees if he does, as soon as you find out, and be with Me!"

## The Real Thing

Approximately four months later, while in clinic, I received a call from my brother in law, who worked at the same large company as my son. He said, "What are you doing at the hospital with Stephen?" I said, "Wait a minute, I'm not at the hospital with Stephen." My brother in law said, "What?" I knew immediately from that call, my son Stephen was at the emergency room, and that could only mean one thing, he had overdosed. I phoned his father immediately to find out if he knew anything, figuring it had to be Stephen's stepmom with him. His father told me Stephen had called him and his speech had been incoherent. Since his father was out of town, he had called Stephen's stepmother to go pick him up. She, in a legitimate panic, drove him immediately to the emergency room. It turned out, Stephen had overdosed in an attic, while on a job as an electrician. By the grace of God, in a total stupor, he stumbled out of the attic and out of the building! Somehow, even though he was totally disoriented, he managed to call his father. However, right after he talked to his father, he was so confused he lost the ability to use his phone. Even though his father tried to call him back, he could not get him, and his father feared for his son's life. As soon as I knew he was at the hospital I hit my knees in prayer. I was at least twenty minutes at best away from him. I was in the middle of seeing patients. As I prayed, I felt a peace come over me that I could not explain. I knew he was alive. This allowed me to finish the patient I was seeing and then go to the hospital.

Stephen remained in ICU for four days because they could not get his blood pressure up, and the doctor feared he might lose his kidneys. By the grace of God, he survived that overdose without any permanent health or organ damage. Praise God! God had more for my son to do!

Since God had given me the "dry run", when Stephen actually overdosed, the first thing I did after I found out he was at the hospital, was hit my knees and prayed. As I said, I was approximately twenty minutes away from him and knew I could not get to my son immediately, but I remembered what God had told me when I experienced my "dry run." I remembered that He said that He would be with Stephen. That day felt very surreal. I felt the presence of My God. I know God was there for me but He was also there for my son. It was a miracle that my son got out of that attic and out of that building. It was a miracle that his stepmother got to him and got him to the hospital rapidly. It was also a miracle that he survived without any kidney or other organ damage. Thank you, God. I know that God helped me through this experience. I was so thankful that since I had spent so much quiet time with Him, I could hear His voice during the "dry run" and knew what to do. I knew to turn to my Heavenly Father who would comfort me in a terrifying situation and give me guidance beyond my understanding.

## God Rest His Soul

Stephen's childhood friend, however, was not so fortunate. Brent and Stephen played together as little boys. I remember them specifically riding on one of those battery-operated three-wheelers among many other memories. Brent had to drive that little three-wheeler with Stephen on the back, because Brent was taller and could reach the handles and peddles. On **June 6, 2017, Richard Brent Jones** died of an overdose after fifteen months of sobriety. **I am so sick and tired of these addictions taking our children.**

**RIP Brent, we will see you soon sweetie, and God Bless his mother, my dear friend,**

**Tina Richards Jones.**

*Amy Shirey PA C, LPC*

# 22

# LET GO LET GOD ONE MORE TIME

## Understanding Codependency

After Stephen's overdose, I took another inventory of myself. Alanon encourages you to do this from time to time. It is the Alanon fourth step, to make sure you are on tract in your recovery. The purpose is to make certain you are fully focused on being healthy and not falling back into codependent behavior. In your inventory you will take an honest look to ensure there is no regression into obsession of your loved one, and there is no one to whom you need to make amends. It is an opportunity to make certain that your focus is not your loved one's recovery, or idolizing your loved one, but on **your** recovery and spiritual growth.

You want to again, take an honest look at what you have done to contribute, if anything, to your loved one's problem, asking yourself in a very genuine, but noncondemning way if you have slipped into "doing for him what he can do for himself". This is done, not for the purpose of condemnation, just to readjust.

I realized thankfully, after Stephen's overdose, that I had not enabled my son. Stephen was not living with me and I had little to no contact with him, only praying for him. I also asked myself honestly the monumental question of, "have I been diligent in my commitment to my daily focus on God?" At the time, I was working and praying for strength and healing. My heart was definitely hurting, but I could feel God's support. So, I felt that I was doing pretty well in that department.

## Continuing your Commitment

I knew I had to continue my devotion to my commitment to God, and make sure my eyes were on Him. This would keep me from spiritual bankruptcy and helped me every day and anytime I went through difficult times. As I continued on my journey after my son's overdose, I remember one day as I was listening to my praise music, and thanking God for saving Stephen from the overdose, a song by Lauren Daigle called, "I Will Trust You" came on the radio. I was singing along with Lauren, when all of a sudden, I began screaming at the top of my lungs, "I will trust You!" over and over. I was thinking that even though Stephen had overdosed which was a close call, I was choosing to **STILL** trust God, and that I would still trust Him with Stephen's life. And I knew God would also help me heal from the pain of my son's overdose. Here is what he revealed to me in the wee hours of the morning, while spending time with Him healing from the overdose.

God clearly said to me, "Amy, I will either bring him home to Heaven, or I will perform a miracle." Obviously, I preferred the latter, but I trusted God's judgement, and I knew it was between Stephen and God, and Stephen's decisions were a part of the equation. I knew I had to face the fact that my son Stephen might very well die from his IV heroin use, but that God and Stephen were in charge of his life, not me. I also knew if God took Stephen home, He would be right there before me, behind me, and inside me, to carry me through that process. I think I could only hear this message from my loving Heavenly Father at this point, because of the many hours that I had spent with Him talking, praying, and just sitting in His presence and feeling His love.

Being a medical practitioner, I knew the stark reality of IV heroin abuse and the high mortality rate. I knew that my son's future was on an extremely dangerous path. Dwelling on this had honestly gotten me into "unbelief land." I had to really hold on to the message that my God gave me that, "He would gently carry him home, or perform a miracle and that it would all be okay." However, I believed that He had a miracle in store for Stephen. As I really had "Let Go", by the grace of God, God and Stephen were to deal with Stephen's life, without my interference.

## Sometimes We Do Witness Miracles...

Tonight, I experienced the promise of a miracle. Stephen, my thirty-two-year-old son and I talked for about fifteen to twenty minutes on the phone, for the first time in years. He has been clean now for approximately nine months. While nine months, in terms of opioid addiction, is really a short term of recovery, it's a miracle that he can use his brain so clearly, in light of the number of years, and amount of drugs, Stephen has used.

We talked about some pretty mature, significant, spiritual matters. Not just "how's the weather" kind of stuff, but things like, opening your heart to Jesus and trusting Jesus as being the only way to heal your broken heart after your parents' divorce. The other miracle that he shared with me was that even though he was already a Christian, he chose to get baptized while living at the half-way house and working through his recovery. I believe all of this was an answer to the many prayers that had been going up for my son. Numerous people had been praying for him. As a matter of fact, there is a church in my community that has one person that comes in and prays every hour. A twenty-four-hour prayer line if you will; and my son was on that list. So, what role did that play in my son's recovery? Well, what do you think? I want that for every mother's child with an addiction! The telephone conversation was a beautifully orchestrated miracle from God. Never give up and always pray for your child with an addiction.

Listen to the song: "Way Maker" by Sinach

*Amy Shirey PA C, LPC*

# 23

# YOU CANNOT PICK THEM BACK UP AGAIN

### Your Job is Done

I had to give my son up to God. I had done all I could do, and it had not worked. In the early years of his addiction, when he was eighteen years old, up to his early twenties, the harder I tried to convince him to get clean, the harder he fought me. Have you ever felt that way?

The alcoholic/addict loves this. He can fight or argue with you, thus avoid fighting the demons within himself. Once you get out of the way, he is left with the miserable feeling within. That is when the real battle begins. It is at that moment that he has no one but himself and the anger and frustration of the disease to battle. This is often when he will turn to God for help. I have talked to mothers who are just starting to face that their child has an addiction and they try to "convince" their child that they have an addiction. This will almost always, especially in the early stages, turn into an argument. Their child will deny that they have a problem until the cows come home! *Please do not argue* with your child!! It can be damaging to your relationship. Just go on your back porch, find a brick wall, and argue your head off with that wall. You will get the same result.

It is ok to tell them you are concerned and that you feel that they have a substance abuse problem. It is ok to enforce consequences for their behaviors, after all, you *are* their parent. I highly recommend you do this the next day when your loved one **is not high or drunk**. You may sit down and say calmly "I am very concerned about your drinking or smoking," or "Because you came home last night with alcohol on your breath you will not be driving your car except to school and back." By the way, neither of these conversations will be pleasant. But…after your declaration, be quiet and let him deal with his feelings of what he did to cause the consequences.

## Your Recovery

Back to my original point of not picking your child back up. When my son reached his late twenties, I had a tendency of letting my son go then when he was in crisis, I'd pick him up again. However, I had made progress on my quiet time with God and having practiced intently on listening for God's voice, I heard God tell me, "Amy, you have done your job. Was your mom still doing all this for you at this age?" The answer was obvious. "No." As I have told you, I was financially and emotionally independent. I was a functioning adult. Unfortunately, when a person has an addictive disease, the disease robs them of normal, as it had with my son. God went on to say, "He's mine now, I am his Heavenly Father, get out of the way, and let Me do My job. Quit interfering." My first thought was that my loud voice in Stephen's head was interfering with God's voice in Stephen's head. If your adult child is a Christian, and he has an addiction, he is probably already battling God's words in his heart and head and that is a good thing. We definitely don't want to get in the way of that.

I recall shortly thereafter, in our little church, a young man who my husband and I did not know, and who did not know our family, came up to my husband and me and said, "I have something to say to ya'll, I see Jesus carrying your son." The young man saw the look of amazement on my face. I had obviously been praying hard for my son. He then said, "You do have a son, right?" We answered in amazement, "Yes, we do! Thank you!" I felt that God had sent me this message of comfort and to confirm His message to "Let Stephen go!" This moment was a breakthrough for me. I was on a mission to deeply understand how to "Let Go and Let God." This message gave me comfort to "Let Go and Let God" carry my son. God could do a much better job than me. I will say again and again, don't be afraid to ask others to pray for your child or adult child with addiction.

Even as your loved one gains sobriety; you may wish you knew her plans for her future. Does she plan to live in the city in which she received treatment, and where her support system is located? Has she met a significant other? Is she going to reconcile with her spouse? As mothers we have a lot of questions often followed by a lot of suggestions. We often justify our "needing to know" because it would "make us feel better" and ease our anxiety. Well, our adult child managing a life/death disease and managing to stay sober is really not about us and keeping us in a feel better state is it? Of course, we would love to hear her announce her plans. Of course, we would love to hear if she has any future dreams, or is that thinking too far ahead? These are all natural, curious questions of a mother, right? But what about a child with an addiction? Her number one priority is her recovery. She is taught to "keep it simple" (life) and take it "one day at a time" (life), as they say in AA. So, as her mom, you need to watch out! Why?

Our loved one's **life** and **her recovery** depend on these concepts and are up to her and God. Her life details will only be given, if she chooses to share. It's called "her boundaries." It can also be a slippery slope for us. It can be a very tempting slippery slope for us to want to suggest, urge, influence, recommend, or manipulate her path without even realizing it. Our relapse into this behavior is just as dangerous as her relapsing into using again. Our relapse into treating her with codependent behavior could actually precipitate her relapse. It would be the old enabling dance we used to do.

You see, if we tell her how to do her life, it makes her feel like a child, helpless and dependent, and oh boy, it triggers our unhealthy power urge, and our trying to get our needs met through our loved one. This is very unhealthy, and it can trigger her as well. Subconsciously, if she has to give us this kind of power, you can bet we are going to pay (that's the basic rule of passive aggression). So how will she make us pay for taking control over her life? She may get us to do a number of things like paying her living expenses, rent, cell phone, car expenses, or raise her children. In addition, she will ask for money (which she will promptly use for drugs or alcohol). You get the picture. Down the toilet we both go. There is no spirituality, no Holy Spirit in that crazy, resentful, chaotic, dance. But I'll tell you who is laughing--the evil one. Unfortunately, this is often what happens when our loved one goes to treatment, gets clean, and returns to a family that has had no education, has not attended Alanon or any treatment (counseling) to understand that they need to work on themselves. The alcoholic is not the only one needing to work on herself.

I hope if this cycle starts, and those old behaviors resurface, that either your loved one or you have had education and are in close personal contact with your loving Heavenly Father and will experience that "yuk" uneasy feeling in your gut and spirit and know that you need to refocus. You see, if you get busy trying to **make** your loved one sober, you can fall into **controlling** a lot of the aspects of her life. These are the areas that we really have no business getting into, so beware, don't go there! You know the drill. These unhealthy behaviors will completely derail our path of healing from our broken heart and put us right back on focusing and perhaps the path of idolizing, our loved ones. Before you know it, our life focus returns to serving our loved one, and not serving God with all our heart and soul.

While working in the medical field, I treated many opioid addicted patients, and I know how difficult it is for these folks to stay clean and sober. I know that all addicts and alcoholics, but particularly IV heroin addicts, are on an extremely dangerous path. But mothers, dwelling on this will not help you. An addiction is an addiction. What you need to hold on to, is the message that your Heavenly Father is in charge and is capable of obliterating any disease. No obstacle is too big for God! You must read and reread

Hebrews and the importance of staying strong and enduring in your faith and make hearing His voice the most important thing in your life.

I cannot pick him back up now. I must continue to work on **My** recovery, and he on his. I must admit that from around the age of seventeen until around the age of twenty-eight, my hyper focusing on his addiction, became an obsession. I learned in Alanon how easy it is to fall back into old patterns. I am not naïve, old habits could re-emerge in us both. We could become toxic with each other. The devil would probably love to see us live under the same roof! It is amazing how after so much prayer and work from us both, the evil one (the devil) would still just love to destroy us! But God is stronger than evil, God is stronger than addiction, God is our protector and refuge!!! We just have to surrender to Him, and walk very close to Him every day!

Listen to the song: "It is Well with My Soul" by Kristene DiMarco

## Healing the Gaping Hole

Recognizing **your** illness, not just your child's, is essential! In that process, your **gaping hole** of pain and scars will need years of the balm of love and healing from God, and is where your focus must remain. But, as you are healing, you too, can help others recognize their obsession and idolization of their loved one with addiction, and see the **gaping hole** in their heart. You can encourage them to turn to God to help them lovingly "Let Go and Let God" take their loved ones to sobriety. Just as Alanon wisely promotes, we can reach out and help others. Remember; our children are not ours; they are a gift from God.

*Children are a heritage from the Lord, offspring a reward from him. (Psalm 127: 3 NIV)*

*Amy Shirey PA C, LPC*

# 24

# SEVENTEEN YEARS
# and
# STILL STANDING ON THE PROMISES

## Court

So here I am, seventeen years after the night my son, age fifteen, sneaked out for his joy ride, sobbing to God. As fear tries to creep in, I am rebuking the devil out of my mind, in Jesus's name, because tomorrow, Stephen, once again, stands before a judge for a felony charge of his past. On the job he stole copper wiring, which he sold for drugs. This is a very common charge for drug users. They take "left over" copper from a construction site, and sell it to get money for drugs. In Stephen's case, he exploited his employer. He has no lawyer. They say he makes too much money at his job to qualify for a public defender even though he has to pay $200.00 per week rent at the half-way house. Since he has no children, he was told he absolutely does not qualify for a public defender. He went to a private attorney's office, and he was told the minimal fee for an attorney's services was thirty-five hundred dollars, which he definitely doesn't have. I'll put my faith in God over an attorney, any day. This I have truly learned.

Now let me stop right here and say that I am not defending his actions of stealing at all. He must absolutely pay the price of his crime. However, wouldn't it make more sense for him to be court ordered to stay in treatment, and pay his prior employer back, instead of going to jail where drugs are readily available, where there is no treatment, and where his current progress will be thwarted? But I am no judge or lawyer, and this is all in God's hands.

But in the midst of this process, I am thinking of the fact that it's ok to ask for a miracle. Right? So, what do I ask? That he gets off? That he stays clean? I've asked that for over sixteen years. No, Father God, I'm going for the big one! I want Stephen to turn his entire life over to You, to want to work and devote his entire being to You and Your service. Because even if he goes to prison and he has dedicated his life to God, he'll be fine. But if the miracle I ask for is for his charges to be dropped, and he is still filled with this evil spirit of addiction, what has that accomplished? If I ask for his sobriety, and he is not devoted to God, well, that is very similar to what I have seen in AA when they talk about "Dry Drunks." These are people who stop using alcohol, but have no peace or serenity, because they have no connection with God. And quite honestly, they often don't stay sober very long.

## Praying for a Miracle and Praising in the Storm

So today, as I lie down on my bed, and the enemy of lies tries to creep into my mind, and frighten me with fears of what can happen to my son if he is locked up again, I jump up in anger, and scream out, "Oh no! Not today devil! Get out of my head, my bed, out of my room, out of my house! I rebuke you in the name of my precious Savior Jesus! God, I trust You! I will trust You! I will trust You! I will trust You! I know You know more than me, and I know You have been with Stephen, You brought him out of the attic when he overdosed, and away from the guy who put a gun in his face. You will rescue him. He is Your child and has lots of people praying for him. I trust You God. I surrender to Your wisdom!"

Listen to "You Are on My Side" by Kim Walker

When your child, who is now an adult, lives on the rollercoaster of addiction, the emotions are there and the only peace is God given. I have felt peace in the midst of the storm and wondered, "How can I feel this?" I knew it was humanly impossible. I knew it had to be from God. Even now, on the eve before he stands before the judge, and believe me, it feels like "we", because my heart will be there standing, I'm reaching up to God for that comfort and peace, and to feel God's love. It's at those times, I'm so glad I've spent so much time "soaking" in my praise music and quiet time just learning how to feel God's love, because now, I know *what* it feels like, and *how* it feels, and I need it so much right now.

A great song to listen to is "I Will Praise You in the Storm" by Casting Crowns.

## Turning to God

My solution, turn to God. It is times such as this when we really need God! Your intimacy with God, your praying on your knees, prepared you for this moment, this crisis. This is when God shows up and shows out for you! And turning to God is exactly what I did that day in the courtroom. I am not saying it looked pretty. I was rocking and I was praying and I was rocking and I was praying. There were tears and there were toes tapping but I kept my faith and well, a funny thing happened.

It turned out that an attorney was in the room that day, that Stephen's dad knew. He agreed to take Stephen's case at a very reduced fee, and Stephen's dad agreed to pay it. Now we will have to await the final answer. Is this enabling? Well, we were not doing for Stephen, what he could do for himself, for sure. He was definitely doing his part in doing his work in his recovery. To help your child and not enable them can be an excruciating decision. I have left Stephen in jail before, but to place him in jail particularly at this time; with Muscogee County Jail publicly stating it has four hundred inmates in gangs and three hundred being in the violent group called Gangster Disciples, this is definitely not a sobriety program.(Ledger Enquirer, Sept. 2017) If you think there are not drugs in jail or prison, think again. But thank God this time Stephen was ready to do his part and was working on his recovery diligently. Stephen agreed to pay his father back while he was in treatment, and he said he had been saving money. We will see, it is still in God's hands.

Now I must say, that helping your child like this can fail miserably. Trust me, I have paid for attorneys before, and my son has promised to pay me back, and I never saw a penny of pay back. It was early in his path of addiction and a part of my learning process, and maybe this is a part of his father's learning curve. I do not know the future. I do know, that Stephen is at a different place in his addiction. For years he denied his disease, then for years he was angry and blamed everyone and everything for his disease. However, when you begin to see your loved one take responsibility for his own behavior and disease, and chose to do what he needs to do to take care of himself, **and you step out of the way and do not interfere,** (all the while focusing on what **you** need to do to heal and grow in your relationship with God), many things change. Yes, God changes things.

## Follow Up

My son faithfully paid his father back and God performed another miracle. Stephen's previous Christian employer, Wade Jordan, of Jordan Electric Company, contacted the attorney Stephen's father secured, and because Stephen was doing so well and had rededicated his life to Christ, Mr. Jordan dropped the charges. God's miracles never cease to amaze. Praise God! Glory be to My Precious Lord and Savior.

# 25

# NEVER GIVE UP!

**You Never Know**

I will never forget hearing in my spirit "the **gaping, hemorrhaging, hole** in a mother's heart" as I felt God tell me to write this book, His book. And I will never forget that feeling of hopelessness, despair, and loss that led me to get down on my face before my Almighty God, which for me, was the only answer for healing my pain. I realized the answer definitely was not throwing money at my child. That was like pouring money down a drain or sieve. In fact, the more money you pour at your child with an addiction, the more dangerous your child's circumstances can become. The answer is also definitely not talking about the addiction ad nauseam. You can nag, lecture, fuss, put your child down, or even feel you are "showing her the light," none of which really work. Hopefully, you have come to realize that you did not cause your child's disease, you cannot cure your child's disease, and you cannot control your child's disease. But, with a close walk and trust in God you can "Let Go and Let God" lead your child into her sobriety. "Letting Go and Letting God" **does not mean giving up on your child**. Did you hear me? **You cannot give up on your child! As a child of God, you always have hope**! Hope for your healing, and faith that your God is greater than your pain, and greater than addiction. He can heal you and your child. You must have enduring belief! I have seen people get sober before that I would never dream would get sober, but by the grace of God, anything can happen!

Listen to the song "One Thing Remains" by Jesus Culture

## Prayer of Enduring Hope for Your Child

Father, I accept that my child has been struggling with an addiction and I have not relied on You, but have tried instead, to fix, cure, or control this situation myself. I ask forgiveness for attempting to handle this on my own. Father I also ask for forgiveness for holding on to any bitterness or anger toward my child. Dear Lord, please release my pain by placing it at the foot of the cross where it belongs, in the name of Jesus Christ. Please Father, I place my precious child in Your arms and pray that she will be delivered to You for Your plans for her life not mine. I will trust in You God that You have plans to care for her, and You have a future for her. I ask Your protection over her. Help me on my journey of healing to turn my eyes toward You, to strengthen my relationship with You, to walk in faith and to yearn to hear Your voice, Lord. Amen.

These steps, along with a deep intimate daily walk with God, will change your life and provide the Peace that surpasses all understanding, regardless of your loved one's condition. You must never give up on your relationship with God getting deeper, and as it does, it will strengthen your faith and the understanding of your loved one's path. Pray for your loved one. Ask God to place "laborers" in her path to speak to her, and to bring her closer to Jesus. Ask other Christians to pray for your loved one and stay very connected and intimate in your walk with your Lord.

## Supplemental Guide

# Creating Intimacy With Your Heavenly Father

Our nation is seeing devastating numbers of our children and adult children being taken hostage by the horrific disease of addiction, and mothers are left with a **hemorrhaging gaping** hole in their heart. The **CREATING INTIMACY** section of this book provides a creative guide on how to begin a daily intimate relationship with your Heavenly Father, which is vital for survival. It will encourage mothers to create a special "Holy Sacred Space," for their intimacy with God and offers creative ideas on how to begin this intimate relationship. In this supplemental section we discuss how to carve out allotted time to "be still and know" that God is always present for you whenever needed, and this reminds mothers that they are not alone. It reminds mothers that "if" they will put the time and effort into their relationship with their Heavenly Father they **will** receive the gifts that their Father promises, gifts of peace, and of understanding and much more.

"Be still and Know" (Psalm 46:10 KJV)

**Creating Intimacy With Your Heavenly Father**

1. Your Holy Sacred Space

2. About Interruptions

3. Let's Talk About Time

4. What Do You Get in Return?

5. Learning to Be Still and Quiet

6. Things You Can Do First

7. You Must Practice

8. Led by the Holy Spirit

9. Going to War

10. Daily Routine

11. Getting Your Peace

## YOUR HOLY SACRED SPACE

Finding your Holy Sacred Space is a very important step; that is why it is the first step. It is the place you are going to commune with God. For some this may feel strange at first, but the goal is that as the relationship develops it will become more and more comfortable. If your relationship with God has previously been cold or distant then think of your Holy Sacred Space as an area that you are creating, to invite in a new special trusted friend.

Start by finding a place in your house or your office. It could be on your porch or maybe even in your garage. You could choose some place as simple as a corner of your bedroom. You can even get fancy, and do as we do in the south, and create yourself a "she shed" or a "man cave" (for dads) in the back yard. It is totally up to you. Just be sure you put some thought into it. It will be your **Holy Sacred Space.** Pray about it. Ask God to help you make this decision. This may sound trivial, but it is not. This will be a place that you will meet with the "Creator of the Universe," your Lord and Savior Jesus Christ, who shed His blood for you. Begin to think of it as a Holy place. A place you want to honor your Lord. You will be inviting the Holy Spirit to join you there in prayer for yourself and others as well as to guide and direct you. It is in this *sacred space* you will be talking to Jesus!

You will be returning to this *space* repeatedly, hopefully for years. Since you will be inviting the presence of the Holy Spirit to join you there, it will be an anointed area, and it will become more and more important and *sacred* to you. So, take some time and think through the details. For example, you may be tempted to pick your porch, but be sure you prepare for different weather conditions. Will you still be able to pray and worship there when it rains? or when it is cold? or when it is extremely hot?

Other considerations include making the best effort to ensure your Holy Sacred Space is quiet. Make sure it is in an area that is protected from distractions, if at all possible. For some, this is next to impossible, and you will have to use additional boundaries. These may include getting up early before the children wake up or enjoying your prayer and praise time after the family has gone to bed. You may even have to plan your quiet time in the middle of the night, and then nap during the day with your small children. If your children are older, teach them about boundaries. Assuming you have taken care of their needs such as dinner and attending to homework, boundaries are a very healthy developmental strategy. Understanding the concept of boundaries can be very helpful in many situations in their lives. Your children should be able to leave you for at least an hour uninterrupted. However, I understand that every family situation is different, and you may need to put dad or perhaps even a sitter in charge for an hour. But try to be creative; this time is essential for you, your spiritual growth, and your sanity. Pray about it, and ask God to help you with answers. He will.

Make your Holy Sacred Space comfortable. Think about some of your favorite comfy items -- a soft comforter, a cozy throw, some pillows, scented candles, special pictures, or a cross. Include anything that is pleasing. I like sunlit windows, Christian music, my Bible close at hand, and my journal. Don't underestimate these items close by that remind you of God's love for you. Some put scriptures on the walls. Some have their pets join them for quiet time. It's also important to survey the area for any objects that have negative energy. You definitely don't want any objects that have non-Christlike origins; a few examples are Buddha statues or tarot cards.

Before using your Holy Sacred Space for the first time, you may want to prayerfully light some incense or essential oils as a way to glorify the area for its blessed purpose. Some may anoint their Holy Sacred Space with oil and pray that the area will be an area of peace and bring them close to their Heavenly Father. They pray that it will be a place that they may commune with God in an open heaven. You can even ask God to send His angels down to praise and celebrate with you in the area that you have adorned for worship. I believe it is very important to return to the same space if at all possible. This ritual shows your commitment to worship and your desire to grow closer to your Heavenly Father.

As you grow in your intimate relationship with your Heavenly Father, your daily quiet time will become as vital to your life as the air you breath. You will need it, want it, and crave it each and every day. There may be days that you just cannot get to your Holy Sacred Space, perhaps you are traveling or working; but it really will not matter because once you have invested time in you sacred space with Him you will learn to hear His voice anywhere! You will be able to hear him on a crowded subway or in your car. This is one of the benefits of developing that closeness and intimacy with your Heavenly Father. The ultimate goal is the relationship, the Holy Sacred Space will just help you get there.

## About Interruptions

It is absolutely imperative that you have no interruptions. If you allow interruptions, you are disrespecting your Heavenly Father and yourself. Don't beat yourself up, but do recognize it as a very vital area of your life that needs work. Many of us mothers, particularly those who have loved ones with addiction, have fallen into the trap of allowing the addict/alcohol to bully us or at least take advantage of us. We often get so "run down" from their constant demands. While in their addictive disease behavior, alcoholics/addicts are manipulative, often to keep the focus off their illness. Even if we are exhausted, we have to work on stopping the interruptions just for this hour. God will give us the strength to fight this evil force of aggression. Your quiet time in this Holy Sacred Space will reverse this exhaustion and fatigue. It will be the place you can regain your strength and receive spiritual restoration.

Remember, the reason you are working to have this time with God is to refill your tank. God has already won this battle against evil aggression. When Jesus rose from the dead, He defeated evil and we do not, as God's children, ever have to bow down to feeling oppressed. Oppression is how we feel when we repeatedly become bullied or taken advantage of by our loved ones with addiction. Beloved, right now you are weary. So…as you start your **quiet time with God,** ask God to fight for you. Just ask him to protect your time together, to prevent any interruptions, and to give you the strength to say "no!"

When your child comes into you Holy Sacred Space and he tries to interrupt your God time, you say, "I can't help you right now; I will get back to you in an hour. Honey, close my door on your way out." Now, I am not naïve enough to think that any child will hear that and just walk out. You will have to repeat that same sentence over and over. You may have to say this two, three, four times, maybe six or seven, but eventually they will get tired of hearing it, get frustrated, and storm out. I repeat, after you have repeated it six to seven times, they **will** get annoyed and walk out because they will realize that nothing else is coming out of your mouth. Make absolutely **no** change in this **UNLESS** someone is bleeding or dying, end of story. So, they whine, "but, momma!" You say, "Are you bleeding? Are you dying?" And when they say, "No," you **repeat,** "I can't help you right now; I will get back to you in an hour and a half" (since they have now taken up more precious God time). "Close the door on your way out. Thank you, sweetie!"

I would also recommend you leave your cell phone in another area of the house and tell your spouse you are going to your Holy Sacred Space to pray. This will hopefully eliminate some interruptions.

## Let's Talk About Time

No one has an hour a day, right? I have felt that way before. At times, I would be really good about taking my hour of quiet time. I would get up early, fix my coffee, and have quiet time with God. As a result, my life was definitely better. Then my child would get sick. After being up two to three nights in a row -- with an earache, of course -- I'd get off track. All of a sudden, everything went to the devil. So, consider your own schedule. Some working moms have their quiet time on their lunch break. Whatever works for you is fine. But whenever you get off track, the important thing to remember is to just get back to it.

The Bible says a righteous man falls down, but he gets back up (Proverbs 24:16 NIV). We go through multiple stages in our lives, and some are easier than others. To stay on a schedule is not always easy. But to consistently stay connected to God in an intimate relationship is priceless. Too often, when things go crazy or things are really bad, we just want to dial Him up and be rescued. Then we wonder why He doesn't fit that fantasy.

A true intimate relationship is about giving and receiving. Our Heavenly Father has already given so much out of the gate! Just look around you at this magnificent world. I'm talking about nature. Take a deep breath. Look at the sunset and the greenery of the trees and the snowcapped mountains...don't get me started again about my love of God's creation. And on top of all that, He gave His precious, loving, nonjudgmental Son who died a criminal's death. So, what have you given back? Can you give an hour a day?

## What Do You Get In Return?

You may not really know what you will get in return for dedicating your time and effort to this intimacy with God, but what do you have to lose? In the Bible, Jesus says, *"'Whoever follows me will never walk in darkness but will have the light of life'"* (John 8:12 NIV). If you have a tiny mustard seed-sized amount of faith that this is true and try this out (devoting your time and heart to this intimate relationship), you stand to gain a lot. You will see that developing this relationship will have a positive return, and as you begin to see the positive results of your intimate relationship with God, your faith will grow. Your faith and the positive results make you want to keep going!

I would like to suggest that you start your first session and perhaps each session of "digging deeper" in your communication with God with this prayer:

*Dear God, I surrender this Holy Sacred Space and my time to You. I ask You to make this a special place for our communication.*

*Please meet me here and clear my mind of all clutter and distractions so that I might grow closer to You.*

*I want to hear You, see You, feel Your presence, and understand just how present You are in my life.*

*Help me God to know how Your presence in me changes my life if I allow it.*

*You know how I have struggled with my loved one having an addiction. I am asking You now to meet me where I am. Help me to surrender to You.*

*Amen.*

## Learning To Be Still And Quiet

After you have found your Holy Sacred Space and made it your own, you have to learn how to be still and quiet within it. Sometimes to be still and quiet is a foreign concept, particularly this day and time. We are inundated with our electronic devices (iPads, iPods, cellphones, TV) and then there is social media; you get the gist. Also, depending on your age (and quite frankly, the number of scars you have accumulated), you may have become very savvy at hiding behind these devices to avoid quiet time. You see, in modern society, it behooves us to become masters at avoiding the *quiet*. When it gets *quiet*, our feelings surface, and uh oh, there comes our emotional pain.

Most of us have heard of the "avoidance theory", but we have basically shrugged our shoulders in regard to it, even when it relates to our children using devices to avoid *their* lives. As a society, we have allowed these distractions even though we are aware that this strategy is detrimental to our relationships to include our marriages, our families, and our relationship with God. There are multiple articles that support that cell phone addictions are damaging our relationships. Just one example was published in *Time Magazine* entitled, "How Your Smartphone is Ruining Your Relationship" written April 28, 2014, by Mandy Oaklander.

Sadly, and unfortunately, but realistically, I suggest if you are very attached or addicted to your phones or devices, you will probably need to start by practicing your quiet time in increments. Try four to five minutes at a time if you need to, and gradually increase in five-minute increments each day as tolerated, that's fine. You may very well have some withdrawal. Coming off of devices is somewhat like coming off a drug for some. Staying on devices many hours a day does a number on your brain chemistry. Therefore, when you stop, your brain chemistry has to make chemical adjustments. To help with this, you can listen to Christian music while sitting still to begin; whatever makes it easier for you. You can read Scriptures, if that helps you, that is fine also. You can also use a white noise sound machine. **Ask God to help you to detoxify from electronic devices**. This will make the withdrawal easier but you may still have some withdrawal which will likely be an eye opener. There are some who use The Twelve Steps of Alanon and apply those as well as prayer to help them come off of their devices.

The whole purpose of quiet time is that you focus inwardly, and you ask God to speak to you and show you what He wants you to see and know. The goal is that eventually you will be able to sit still and quiet for an hour allowing yourself to hear God's voice. Does this mean you are going to hear an audible voice outside yourself? Not necessarily, although some people do. God speaks to us through The Holy Spirit. The Holy Spirit speaks to us in various ways. He may speak to you through Scripture, or the "quiet still voice" in the night (1 Kings 19:11-13 KJV). He may come to you as a "knowing." He may speak to you through nature or a dream. Be alert and open to Him. This takes time and patience, two things in short supply today. However, the rewards are priceless. Some people absolutely cannot tolerate silence in the beginning, so they start off just reading the Bible. The Bible is God's Word and He can speak to you straight from His Word.

I think about the phenomenal amount of time, energy, and practice that is required by people who run marathons. My parents used to tell me that anything really worth doing takes hard work and dedication. Well, I know that my relationship with God and hearing the voice of God has taken diligence and time but the outcome has been life changing and has provided an anchor that will stabilize me the rest of my life no matter what I face.

## Things You Can Do First

To get started on your journey of closeness to God, you may find it extremely helpful to purchase your own personal journal. You can write a heartfelt letter to God explaining where you are in your life and why you are coming to Him at this juncture. A journal is an excellent place to keep your prayer requests and answered prayers. You may just write a free-lance narrative from your heart and soul to your Heavenly Father. You can take this opportunity to write a letter of confession to God expressing any deep regret or sorrow you may feel for things you have done, then you can get down on your knees and ask for forgiveness. This can offer healing.

One powerful way to use your journal is to write a letter of all the things you are angry or bitter about and then ask God to help you work through them. The anger and bitterness are often just the top layer. You may realize as you journal, that you have feelings of betrayal or hurt deep down below this anger and as you explore with God those hurts and betrayals, He will lead you to a need to forgive others who have hurt you. You may also uncover feelings of unresolved grief below your bitterness. It can be very helpful to share that sadness with your Heavenly Father who definitely understands and will comfort you. God will lead you and help you. These are wonderful ways to help you heal when added to prayer and reading God's Word.

Writing in a journal can help you see things that you didn't even realize were present in your heart and soul that need to be talked about with your Heavenly Father. Regardless of how you communicate with God, be it a journal or verbally, it is just important that you start. Often writing in a journal or praying to God out loud keeps us from getting distracted. As you begin to open your heart and begin to become vulnerable with God, He will befriend you, just as He did Abraham. (James 2:23 NIV) He will comfort you and He will help you come to a greater understanding of how to heal from all your pain.

Our God is a compassionate God. He already knows our pain, our thoughts, and our sins. Communication with Him is key. He is more than willing to meet us halfway. We just have to be still and quiet, long enough to be available to Him. Whatever your personal approach of connecting with God, it will be pleasing to Him. There are no wrong ways to communicate with Him.

Just take note, that if while working on this intimate communication, you hear condemnation, persecuting thoughts, put downs, or criticism come into your mind, that is **not coming from God**. Those are the lies from the enemy (Romans 8:1 NIV). That is Satan trying to discourage you! He gets very nervous when God's children get really obedient and close to their Father. Just whisper a quiet prayer asking God to remove those lies from your mind. Or, when you are feeling stronger, stand up and demand the devil to take a hike! In the name of Jesus. You can declare that you are a child of God and he has **NO POWER OVER YOU**! Demand him to get out of your head, out of your sacred space, out of your home, in the name of Jesus!

## YOU MUST PRACTICE

Having your time with The Lord (God, Jesus and the Holy Spirit) repeatedly has such a benefit that is even difficult to explain, but will definitely be experienced. Your intimacy with God will strengthen your trust in God, your feelings of protection by God, and your feelings of being loved by God. Over time, it will also make you more aware of your ability to feel the presence of the Holy Spirit within you.

Let me take a minute here to discuss the obvious. As Christians we believe in the Holy Trinity, meaning that God is three, God, Jesus, and the Holy Spirit (Matthew 28:19, Luke 3:22, John 14:26, John15:26 NIV). In your quiet time you may be praying to God, or sometimes you may pray for Jesus to help you, it doesn't matter it goes to the same address. God communicates with you through the Holy Spirit who came to us on earth when Jesus ascended to Heaven after He arose from the grave. Jesus left the Holy Spirit to help us Christians, and boy do we need the Holy Spirit! We have the Holy Spirit in our hearts to comfort and guide us, among other things that the Holy Spirit does. Only a Christian who has asked Jesus into their heart and life has the privilege of help from the Holy Spirit and can feel Him. The Holy Spirit comes into our heart when we surrender our hearts to Jesus.

As you begin to do your daily quiet time with God, more benefits arise. You will begin to feel that you can really lean on God, depend on Him, and know that He is there for you. He will comfort you, and protect and provide for you. The more you give to the relationship through prayer, worship, and listening to God in quiet time, the more the relationship deepens. The amazing thing that slowly happens is that you start feeling **joy,** and with this **joy** you actually feel your **strength** coming back. This is the **restoration** that can only come from God. This is **the missing key** of surviving your child's addiction. This is what makes you want more closeness and intimacy with God. This is what lets you know that with God you can survive.

In addition to your quiet time, as I have mentioned earlier in this book, I believe it is very helpful to also have a spiritual support group, a group of believers who have developed their own closeness with God and who understand the need for God in their life on a deep level. This is especially helpful if you are a young Christian. This may be in the form of a Bible study and hopefully a home church. It can be very helpful to find a small Christian prayer group.

What worked for me, was finding a Bible study of loving nonjudgmental Christian women, and at first, God led me to a small non-denominational Spirit filled church. I really believe that God led me to both. He knows what you need and He will lead you to just the right place and the right people if you ask for Him to help you. Pray for it! Ask Him to lead you to these support groups and people. Get out and try some churches. Think about your circle of friends and ask them if any are interested in starting a prayer group, especially if you have a friend with a child with an addiction. Trust your inner feelings about the reception you receive as you do these things. God will let you know if it is the place for you. He will send you a sign.

Often it is a sign of peace when you are in the right place or approaching the right people. Don't sit around in pain and silence. If you are seeking God, He knows what you need and will guide you to the answers to truth you are seeking, and He will help you to the right people and places in your life. (Philippians 4:19 NIV)

## Led By The Holy Spirit

As we honestly and genuinely seek God in our Holy Sacred Space and quiet time, some very miraculous things begin to happen. We do begin to feel some changes. I remember being at the point of complete vulnerability. I had basically surrendered to God because well, I couldn't function anymore on my own. Actually, that was when I talked to Him sincerely and consistently every day several times per day and that is when I felt the change. He took charge of me because I couldn't take charge of myself anymore.

I'm not talking about that vulnerability that we mothers feel when our whole life feels out of control and our loved one is spinning into the pit of despair due to his addiction. No, that is when we are hopelessly entangled in chaos, pain, and destruction caused by the evil one. I learned as long as I stayed there, not only was I a "basket case" but there was no hope.

But instead, I am talking about the point after I had made the difficult decision to put my child in the arms of God and put my eyes on Jesus. I still felt vulnerable and hurt after all the pain, like a little child lost in the woods walking around aimlessly, but God took my hand and said "Don't worry my child, I've got you." I still felt weak, but because I was **faithfully working on my relationship with God**, by talking with Him daily, I could feel His protection and knew He was there carrying me. I used my quiet time every day to visualize walking in the forest hand in hand with God, at first with my broken heart, but I knew He was my protector and provider. It was such a comfort. As time passed, I felt the heaviness lift and my strength and joy slowly return.

I just kept my eyes on God in trust, and His gift, which is Christ Jesus, His Son. At times I could hear a voice within, obviously the Holy Spirit, healing and guiding me through adversity (John 14:16 NIV). But I remembered, as long as I stayed focused on God and His gift of salvation, I could survive anything with the peace that surpasses all understanding (Philippians 4:7 NIV).

Once you believe in God and Jesus as His Son, and ask Them to come in your heart, The Holy Spirit takes up residency in your heart and soul, and it's a *sealed* deal. Then the Holy Spirit becomes very busy!

- He will be with you at all times, that means; when you are vulnerable, He will comfort you but it also means the Holy Spirit is ALWAYS with you, and:

- He will pray for you when you are too tired or weary to pray, or when you just don't know any more how or what to pray.

- He will guide you toward what God wants you to do, IF you allow Him, ask Him, and if you listen to Him, He will tell you.

- The Holy Spirit will tell you if you are heading in the wrong (ungodly) direction, if you listen, He will tell you.

- He knows God's desires for your life.

- The Holy Spirit is God ("The Father, Son and Holy Ghost ").

- The Holy Spirit will give you strength.

- The Holy Spirit will help you understand the Bible.

Wow that's a lot, and if you really work hard on this relationship, you can get really adept at hearing His voice.

## GOING TO WAR (During Your Intimacy)

All of the things above (the things the Holy Spirit does for us) really comes in handy when you go to spiritual war against the enemy and that is an understatement. When your child or adult child or spouse has an addiction, it feels like an attack by the devil on your loved one and your family, because it is! Satan loves to use addiction to slip into your families and wreak havoc. This is spiritual warfare and nothing can be used to battle this except the power of the Holy Spirit. Here are the steps:

First Remember: Jesus died a criminal's death and hung on a Cross but He rose from the dead defeating death and sin! And because He lives and will be seated at the right hand of God, He is King of Kings over all including Satan. We were told by Jesus that as Christians we are God's children and heirs to God's kingdom, and that because of that, Satan has NO power over us. So, when Satan comes strolling around our children, we have every authority to denounce, declare, or make a decree to bound him up and send him to the foot of the cross in the powerless position that he belongs (Matthew16:19 NIV). Christ already won the victory over evil. We just have to take the authority given to us through Christ to go up against the evil one as prayer warriors for our children who are under attack.

In Luke 10:19, Jesus said that we have the same authority over evil as He does. It is ours for the taking but we must **believe in our authority through Christ.**

1. Put on the armour of God for protection. (Ephesians 6:10-18 NIV) Put it on your loved one, and yourself!

2. And in the authority given to you through Jesus Christ, command the spirit of evil out of your loved one in Jesus's name, and as said earlier, out of your mind, and your home in Jesus's name!

If your loved one is a Christian, he has the Holy Spirit within, and he cannot be demon possessed, but he may be tortured by evil spirits. He may have some evil spirits within from using, the devil uses the drugs as a port of entry. Those can be bound on earth and heaven and sent to the foot of the Cross in the name of Jesus (Matthew18:18 NIV). If your loved one is not a believer, pray fervently and fast for him. Ask other Christians to pray and fast diligently for his soul to be saved.

We mothers need to band together as prayer warriors for our children and adult children. In prayer we can bind these evil spirits away from our children and adult children in Jesus's name. The devil is working overtime to seduce our kids, and we need, as Christian mothers to put on our war gear and go to battle for them. Our cities and nations need our Christian mothers to join hands in prayer as warriors against the evil one trying to take our children.

## Daily Routine

You don't have to use this daily routine. You can develop your own, but if you want, this can be a "starter routine."

Meet with God at least once a day for 15-30 minutes. Work up to an hour.

Start with a favorite Christian song of praise. (one of my favorites: Elevation Worship. "Here Again." *Hallelujah Here Below.* Elevation Church, 2018. album.)

Then say the prayer I suggested (page 161) or use your own.

Confess to God any sin you have committed (anything that you feel you have done wrong to hurt another) and ask for forgiveness.

Open your heart about your concerns--you might want to write in a prayer journal the date and any concerns you have so that you can write down when those concerns vanish, to see prayers answered.

Write down what you are asking for in your journal, be sure to include "a growth of faith and closeness to Him."

Then for the last ten minutes, put on soft music or be silent and tell God you want to devote time to listening to what He has to say to you and what He wants from you.

Close in prayer and thanksgiving for what He has done for you, the abundance He continues to send you and His unrelentless love and protection.

## Getting Your Peace (In Your Holy Sacred Space)

I want to leave you with this… not only will you get peace as you spend quiet time with God, He will renew your excitement about life. When you get closer to your Heavenly Father, and take the risk of opening yourself up to Miracles, it's exciting.

As mothers or parents of addicts we can sure use a little excitement, even a little happiness. I remember as I began to heal, even though I was feeling a little vulnerable, one of my Christian friends, Sonya, took me to an event in North Georgia where a Bible was producing "Holy oil." It was a supernatural event. Well, I was skeptical of course, growing up in a "religiously stiff" environment. However, I attended. They prayed for me, and actually a young girl named Jen prayed for me and prophesied over me that I would successfully write this book. But the most important thing that the trip did for me was, it opened my mind to remembering God's possibilities. Anything is possible with God. Don't limit Him! He wants to help you and He is the "God of Miracles."

Listen to the song: "Miracles" (Live) featuring Chris Quilala
Jesus Culture. "Miracles." *Let it Echo.* Sparrow, 2016. Album.

*Amy Shirey PA C, LPC*

# END NOTES

**Chapter 1**
1.) Jobe, Kari. "I Am Not Alone." *Majestic*. Sparrow, 2014. Album.

**Chapter 2**
1.) Elevation Worship. "O Come to The Altar." *Here as in Heaven*. Elevation, 2017. Album.

**Chapter 3**
1.) I Am They. "Scars." *Trial and Triumph*. Sony Music Provident, 2016. Album.

**Chapter 4**
1.) West, Matthew. "Out of My Hands." *Happy*. Universal South, 2002. Album.

**Chapter 5**
1.) American Psychiatric Association: *Diagnostic and Statistical Manual of Mental Disorders,* Fourth Edition, Text Revision. Washington, DC, American Psychiatric Association, 2000.
2.) Morse, RM; Flavin, DK (August 26, 1992). "The definition of alcoholism, The Joint Committee of the National Council on Alcoholism and Drug Dependence and the American Society of Addiction Medicine to Study the Definition and Criteria for the Diagnosis of Alcoholism". *The Journal of the American Medical Association*. 268 (8): 11012-4.
3.) Battistelli, Francesca. "Giants Fall." *If We're Honest*. Word Entertainment and Fervent Records, 2014. Album.

**Chapter 6**
1.) Daigle, Lauren. "You Say." *Look Up Child*. Centricity, 2019. Album.

**Chapter 7**
1.) Narcotics Anonymous (NA) A twelve-step program to help people gain sobriety for those addicted to narcotics as opposed to Alcoholics Anonymous (AA) which is a twelve-step program to help people to gain sobriety for those addicted to alcohol.

2.) Wickham, Phil. "How Great is Your Love." *Living Hope.* Fair Trade Services, 2018. Album.

**Chapter 8**

1.) Weave, Big Daddy. "Redeemed." *Love Com to Life.* Fervent Records, 2012. Album.

**Chapter 9**

1.) American Psychiatric Association: *Diagnostic and Statistical Manual of Mental Disorders,* Fourth Edition, Text Revision. Washington, DC, American Psychiatric Association, 2000.

**Chapter 10**

1.) We Are Messengers." Maybe It's Ok." *Maybe It's Ok.* Mulligan Records, 2018. Album.

**Chapter 11**

1.) Hall, Mark. "Come to the Well." *Come to the Well.* Beach Street and Reunion Records, 2011. Album.

**Chapter 12**

1.) Sarah Young, *Jesus Calling (*Nashville, TN.: Thomas Nelson of Harper Collins Christian Publishing 2004).

2.) Daigle, Lauren. "Rescue." *Look Up Child.* Centricity, 2019. Album.

**Chapter 13**

1.) Redman, Matt. "Gracefully Broken." *Gracefully Broken.* Capitol Studio, 2017. Album.

2.) Jobe, Kari. "Speak to Me." *The Garden.* Sparrow KAJE, 2017. Album.

**Chapter 14**

1.) Hillsong. "Surrender." *Cornerstone.* Hillsong, Capitol, Sparrow, 2012. Album.

2.) Francesca Battistelli. "Lead Me to the Cross." *My Paper Heart.* Fervent, Curb, 2008. *Album.*

3.) West, Matthew. "Only Grace." *History.* Universal South, 2005. Album.

**Chapter 15**

   1.) Williams, Zack. "Fear is a Liar." *Chain Breaker*. Essential, 2016. Album.

   2.) Priscilla Shirer, Fervent: A Woman's Battle Plan for Serious, Specific, and Strategic Prayer (Nashville, TN: B & H Publishing Group, 2015)

   3.) Smith, Taya. "Oceans (Where Feet May Fall)." *Zion*. Hillsong Capitol, 2019. Album.

**Chapter 16**

   1.) West, Matthew. "The Motions." *Something to Say*. Sparrow, 2009. Album.

   2.) Casting Crowns. "Just Be Held." *Thrive*. Beach Street & Reunion Records, 2014. Album.

**Chapter 17**

   1.) Francesca Battistelli. "He Knows My Name." *If We Are Honest*. Word Entertainment and Fervent Records, 2014. Album.

   2.) Springer, Rita. "Defender." *Battles*. Gateway Music, 2017. Album.

**Chapter 18**

   1. Crowder, David. "Come as You Are." *Neon Steeple*. Sparrow, 2014. Album.

   2. Daigle, Lauren. "Remember." *Look Up Child*. Centricity, 2019. Album.

**Chapter 19**

   1.) Jobe, Kari. "The Garden." *The Garden*. Sparrow KAJE, 2017. Album.

**Chapter 20**

   1.) Third Day. "Cry Out to Jesus." *Wherever You Are*. Essential Records, 2005. Album.

**Chapter 22**

   1.) Daigle, Lauren. "Trust in You." *How Can it Be?* Centricity, 2016. Album.

   2.) Joseph, Osinachi. "Way Maker." *Waymaker-Live*. Loveworld SLIC, 2016. Album.

**Chapter 23**

1.) DiMarco, Kristene. "It is Well with My Soul." *Mighty*. Jesus Culture Music, Sparrow, 2015. Album.

**Chapter 24**

1.) Walker, Kim. "You Are on My Side." *On My Side*. Jesus Culture Music, Sparrow, 2017. Album.

2.) Casting Crowns. "I will Praise You in the Storm." *Lifesong*. Beach Street and Reunion Records, 2005. Album.

3.) Williams, C., (2017, September, 07), Gangster disciples is largest street gang in Columbus according to police sheriff. *The Ledger Enquirer,* p.4A

**Chapter 25**

1.) Jesus Culture. "One Thing Remains." *Come Away*. Jesus Culture Music, 2010. Album.

Amy Shirey is available for book interviews and personal appearances. For more information contact:

Amy Shirey
C/O Advantage Books
P.O. Box 160847
Altamonte Springs, FL 32716
info@advbooks.com


To purchase additional copies of these books, visit our bookstore at:
www.advbookstore.com

Longwood, Florida, USA
"we bring dreams to life"™
www.advbookstore.com

Made in the USA
Columbia, SC
14 September 2020

20735850R00098